Superfood Breakfasts!

50 Smoothie Bowls, Power Bars & Energy Balls

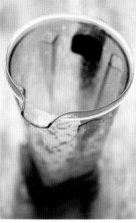

Superfood
Breakfasts!

50 Smoothie Bowls, Power Bars & Energy Balls

Sara Lewis

PHOTOGRAPHY BY WILLIAM SHAW

LORENZ BOOKS

This edition is published by Lorenz Books,
an imprint of Anness Publishing Ltd,
108 Great Russell Street, London WC1B 3NA;
info@anness.com

www.lorenzbooks.com; www.annesspublishing.com;
twitter:@Anness_Books

Publisher: Joanna Lorenz
Photography: William Shaw
Food for photography: Sara Lewis
Designer: Adelle Mahoney
Styling: Pene Parker
Editorial: Sarah Lumby

COOK'S NOTES

Bracketed terms are intended for American readers.
For all recipes, quantities are given in both metric
and imperial measures and, where appropriate, in
standard cups and spoons. Follow one set of
measures, but not a mixture, because they
are not interchangeable.
Standard spoon and cup measures are level.
1 tsp = 5ml, 1 tbsp = 15ml, 1 cup = 250ml/8fl oz.
Australian standard tablespoons are 20ml.
Australian readers should use 3 tsp in place of
1 tbsp for measuring small quantities.
American pints are 16fl oz/2 cups. American readers
should use 20fl oz/2.5 cups in place of 1 pint when
measuring liquids.
Electric oven temperatures in this book are for
conventional ovens. When using a fan oven, the
temperature will probably need to be reduced by
about 10–20°C/20–40°F. Since ovens vary, you
should check with your manufacturer's instruction
book for guidance.
The nutritional analysis given for each recipe is
calculated per portion (i.e. serving or item), unless
otherwise stated. If the recipe gives a range, such as
Serves 4–6, then the nutritional analysis will be for
the smaller portion size, i.e. 6 servings. The analysis
does not include optional ingredients, such as
salt added to taste.
Medium (US large) eggs are used unless
otherwise stated.

PUBLISHER'S NOTE

Although the advice and information in this book
are believed to be accurate and true at the time of
going to press, neither the author nor the publisher
can accept any legal responsibility or liability for any
errors or omissions that may have been made nor
for any inaccuracies nor for any loss, harm or injury
that comes about from following instructions or
advice in this book. The reader should not regard
the recommendations, ideas and techniques
expressed and described in this book as substitutes
for the advice of a qualified medical practitioner or
other qualified professional. Any use to which the
recommendations, ideas and techniques are put is
at the reader's sole discretion and risk.

Contents

10 minutes to change your life!

Packed with superfoods such as kale, spinach, blueberries, flaxseeds, nuts, yogurt and wholegrains, smoothie bowls, jars and bars are the super-trendy way to start the day. For a visual and nutritional boost add exotic nutrition-packed toppings such as crispy and crunchy homemade granola, maple-glazed seeds and scatterings of jewel-like pomegranate seeds or goji berries.

These fabulous breakfast ideas not only look good but do you good too. We should all be eating more fruit and vegetables and these are just bursting with essential vitamins, minerals, good fats, good carbs and fibre to help keep our body in tip-top shape, to boost our immunity, fight fatigue and help to protect us from cancer, heart disease, obesity and diabetes. Those who eat breakfast tend to have more balanced diets than those who skip it, and are less likely to be overweight, lose weight more successfully, and reduce their risk of ill health. Chances are if you miss breakfast you will be more likely to snack on less healthy foods or eat a much larger lunch. If you feel you just don't have time for breakfast, set the alarm clock 15 minutes earlier, or prepare your basic ingredients beforehand and keep in the refrigerator ready to serve out and add a topping just before you eat.

First up are energy bowls, brightly coloured nutrient-packed blends that can be served hot or cold. Porridge gets a makeover with summer berries, blackberries and bananas, or try combinations of quinoa, beetroot and orange; a lentil dhal topped with spiced cauliflower and kale; black rice with papaya; and edamame beans mixed with miso, ginger, kale and broccoli.

The quick and easy fruit and vegetable soups are super-healthy blends of great-tasting ingredients – whizz up green tea, mango and lime, or avocado and garden peas – all with crunchy toppings to energize and keep you powered through the morning.

Smoothie bowls just shout out goodness, blending action-packed ingredients for maximum flavour and nutrition. Top your bowl as you like, depending on what you have in the cupboard, refrigerator or freezer. Build up a larder of nutrient-boosting ingredients bit by bit and keep a handy supply of frozen ready-prepared fruits for those days when you don't have time, or fresh supplies are running low. Adding a mix of fresh and frozen fruits will give your smoothie bowl the most delicious ice cream-like texture that is hard to resist.

The easy and fashionable way to eat on the go is the glass jar packed with tempting healthy layers, ready to pop into your bag to take to work or the gym. Avocado, kale, pea shoots, mango, beetroot and apple are blended or shredded and layered over homemade muesli and granola, and topped with yogurt, cashew creams and nutritional boosters.

The chapter on healthy power balls, low-fat flapjacks and muesli bakes gives you instant energy in your pocket to keep you going for breakfast or as a pick-me-up later on in the day.

FOR A HEALTHY BREAKFAST AIM TO INCLUDE

1 Good carbs from healthy wholegrains such as oats, quinoa and rice. They will help kick-start your metabolism and are low in fat.
2 Fruit and vegetables rich in antioxidants, vitamins, minerals and fibre. Choose from fresh or frozen.
3 Protein from nuts, seeds and wholegrains.
4 Healthy fats from nuts, seeds, avocado, or choose olive, hemp, avocado or nut oil.

Eat a rainbow

Fruit and vegetables come in an amazing array of colours and sizes. Eating a variety of foods is the key to a healthy diet and what better way than to include lots of vegetables and fruit in your daily breakfast smoothie bowl.

Health professionals recommend that we eat at least five portions of vegetables and fruit a day, with some suggesting that we should be ideally aiming for seven to eight portions, yet many of us don't even manage three or four. Rich in cancer-protecting antioxidants, many of which give the fruit and vegetables their deep colours, as well as vitamins, minerals, carbs and fibre, this huge food group can also help to protect against heart disease, obesity and diabetes.

Adding fruit and vegetables to smoothie bowls and warming energy-boosting porridge, layering them with yogurt, or stirring them into muesli bars or power balls, is a really proactive and easy way to boost your intake.

GREEN

Broccoli – the darker the florets, irrespective of them being green, deep blue-green or purple, the higher the amounts of vitamin C and beta-carotene which the body converts into vitamin A. Broccoli also contains beneficial indoles – nitrogen compounds which may help to protect DNA from damage and so protect against cancer.

Cabbage – try also collard greens or spring greens. They are all rich in vitamin C, E and K, plus folates required for cell division and the formation of DNA, along with potassium for fluid balance and to help regulate blood pressure. They also contain indoles. Use cabbage sparingly in smoothie bowls as the flavour can be a little overpowering.

Herbs – choose from parsley, coriander/cilantro, mint and basil for a chlorophyll-boosting, detoxing addition to smoothies. Parsley contains useful amounts of vitamin C and iron and can help as a breath freshener while mint aids digestion and also freshens breath. Coriander aids digestion and adds a spicy fresh tang to any smoothie. Basil acts as a natural tranquilizer and is thought by herbalists to calm the nervous system, aid digestion and ease stomach cramps.

Lettuce – choose darker green leaves for the most nutritional value. As the leaves have such a high water content, calories are low. Amounts of vitamin C and K vary between types of lettuce with romaine lettuce having some of the highest amounts.

Kale – like broccoli, whatever the variety, the darker the leaves the higher amounts of vitamin C they contain. Kale also has vitamin B and K, chlorophyll and iron which helps with the oxygenation and health of blood cells, so helping to fight fatigue. It also contains the antioxidant lutein which may help to protect from macular eye degeneration, indoles which may protect against oestrogen-related cancers, and sulforaphane which helps the liver to detoxify carcinogenic compounds. Buy as whole leaves or bags of ready-shredded to save time.

Sea vegetables – seaweed is packed with nutrition. It is rich in iodine needed for normal functioning of the thyroid gland, with smaller amounts of copper and iron for healthy blood, magnesium for proper functioning of muscles and nerves, calcium for healthy bones, potassium for the balance of fluids, and zinc for the body's immune system. Seaweed can be bought dried and ready-shredded in small packs – look for mixed sea vegetables that include dulce, nori and sea lettuce. There is no need to soak in water before use, simply add a spoonful to a smoothie bowl when blending.

Spinach – this is packed with a high concentration of carotenoids, including beta-carotene and lutein which may help protect against cancer. It also contains potassium and folates. Choose baby spinach leaves as they are lower in oxalates; as the leaves grow in size so the amount of oxalates increase and this can inhibit the absorption of calcium and iron from the spinach. When added to smoothie bowls, spinach blends to an ultra-smooth purée with a delicate flavour that doesn't overpower berries and other fruits. You might also like to try Swiss chard with their white stems or rainbow chard with their vibrant muti-coloured stems.

Apples – choose apples with green or red skins for natural energy-boosting sweetness. The pectin they contain helps to lower cholesterol and helps to activate beneficial bacteria in the

WHAT ARE ANTIOXIDANTS?

Antioxidants are one of the first lines of defence that the body employs, to keep free radicals that occur during oxidation from damaging cells, and to help repair the harm that they do. Cells undergoing oxidative stress that contain DNA have been linked to serious illnesses such as cancer, heart disease, stroke, Parkinson's disease, Alzheimer's, autoimmune diseases, cognitive decline and macular degeneration.

There are many natural antioxidant compounds in fruit and vegetables but the most common dietary ones are beta-carotene which is used by the body to make vitamin A, vitamin C and vitamin E; plus anthocyanins in blueberries; flavonoids found in tea, red wine and citrus fruits; indoles found in cruciferous vegetables such as broccoli, cabbage and cauliflower; lignans in seeds; lutein in leafy greens; and lycopene in tomatoes and pink grapefruit, along with the minerals zinc, selenium and copper.

large intestine, while adding vitamin C and boosting fibre.

Avocado – thought to be one of the most nutritionally complete fruits, avocados are rich in concentrated energy in the form of mono-unsaturated fats, plus vitamin B6 needed to aid energy release. They have more potassium than bananas, which helps regulate blood pressure and lower the risk of heart attacks and strokes, and they are rich in vitamin E with smaller amounts of vitamin C and lutein to help protect against macular degeneration. Avocados add a wonderful velvety creaminess to smoothie bowls; try drizzling a little avocado oil over the top too.

Green grapes – fresh, tangy and a good source of potassium to help regulate blood pressure, grapes add a natural sweetness to smoothie bowls and are only 60 calories per 100g/3¾oz.

Kiwi fruit – packed with immune-boosting vitamin C and a good source of potassium they also contain the antioxidant lutein which may help to protect against macular degeneration. The little black seeds are a good source of soluble fibre which can also help to lower blood cholesterol.

YELLOW AND ORANGE

Carrots – these really do help you see in the dark, as the beta-carotene they contain is converted to vitamin A in the body which helps our eyes adjust quickly to changes in light. In traditional medicine carrots were known for their detoxifying properties. Their high levels of vitamin A are also thought to fight the signs of ageing by nourishing the skin and helping to fight wrinkles.

Corn – naturally sweet and packed with complex carbs and fibre for a slow-release energy boost.

Sweet potatoes – like corn this vegetable is naturally sweet and can be added to smoothies and cakes to help reduce the need for added sugar. They contain vitamins A and C, fibre and potassium, plus useful amounts of magnesium and manganese.

Yellow (bell) peppers – all peppers are rich in vitamin A, C and K. These vitamins help to prevent cell damage, cancer and diseases related to ageing.

Mango – rich in natural energy-boosting fruit sugars plus beta-carotene and vitamin C.

Oranges, lemons, limes and grapefruit – are all rich in vitamin C to help boost our immune system and to aid the absorption of iron. Pink grapefruit and blood oranges also contain good amounts of beta-carotene while lemons contain limonene, a phytochemical that is thought to help protect against cancer.

Papaya – this fruit contains the enzyme papain which is similar to pepsin produced during digestion, so helping to soothe your tummy. It is rich in vitamin C, plus beta-carotene with smaller amounts of calcium and iron.

Pineapple – full of natural sugars, vitamin C and the digestive enzyme bromelain which can have a calming effect on the stomach. It is also thought to have anti-inflammatory properties.

RED

Cherries – rich in beta-carotenes and potassium, cherries have anti-inflammatory properties and may be beneficial for those suffering with gout and arthritis.

Cranberries – most well-known for helping to prevent urinary tract infections, cranberries are rich in antioxidants and may help protect against cancer and heart disease; they may even help prevent mouth ulcers and have anti-ageing properties.

Goji berries – these tiny bright red fruits are brimming with beta-carotene, and also contain vitamin C, antioxidants and fibre.

Tomatoes – rich in lycopene, a carotenoid pigment that turns them red and that is thought to help prevent against some forms of cancer. Tomatoes are also a good source of potassium, with smaller amounts of vitamin A, C and E. They contain 90% water so are also good for rehydration.

Raspberries – as well as vitamin C, raspberries also contain manganese which helps with the metabolism of carbs, proteins and cholesterol and aids good bone health.

Strawberries – with more vitamin C than any other red berry, these also have great antiviral and antibacterial properties. Rich in beta-carotene they also contain lignin which may help reduce blood cholesterol. Naturally sweet, they also help boost energy.

Watermelon – with its high water content,

watermelon helps to rehydrate and plump your skin. It also contains the antioxidant glutathione, which is thought to help boost the immune system and fight infection. Like tomatoes, watermelon gets its colour from lycopene.

PURPLE

Beetroot – this vegetable has one of the highest sugar levels of any vegetable, great for boosting energy. It also contains folates, vitamin C and potassium with small amounts of iron. The high levels of nitrates are thought to benefit sportsmen and women and may even help slow the progression of dementia. Beetroot also contains the antioxidant group of betalains.

Blackberries – a good source of vitamin C, folates and fibre. They also contain salicylates, a natural asprin-like compound.

Blueberries – packed with antioxidants called flavonoids these may help to protect against cancer, premature ageing, heart disease and degenerative diseases caused by oxidative stress. They are also rich in vitamin C, natural fruit sugars and pectin to help lower cholesterol, plus they act as an anti-inflammatory.

Plums – a good source of vitamin C, but don't eat in very large quantities as they can have a laxative effect.

Pomegranate – these tiny red seeds are packed with fibre and also contain vitamins A, C and E plus iron.

WHITE

Bananas – this is the only fruit to contain tryptophan, plus vitamin B6 which together helps the body to produce serotonin, making it the natural good-mood food. Rich in fruit sugars and starch, bananas boost energy while the potassium they contain helps to regulate blood pressure.

Cauliflower – this rather old-fashioned vegetable has staged a comeback as the sulphurous compounds it contains may help to protect against cancer. It also contains vitamin C.

Pears – like apples, pears contain natural fruit sugars, which are absorbed more slowly by the body than refined sugars. Pears are also rich in pectin to help lower cholesterol.

DON'T FORGET ABOUT DRIED FRUIT

These make handy store-cupboard standbys: sprinkle dried cranberries or goji berries over a smoothie or add to a trail mix topping or mix into homemade granola. Layer diced dried apricots with extra fresh fruit and yogurt, or add to fruit smoothies or soups to add sweetness. Add figs and prunes to power balls or flapjack-style bakes, or stir into yogurt. As the fruits are dried their nutritional content is super-concentrated, but so too is their sugar content, so add in small quantities.

Fruity freezer

While we all think fresh is best, frozen is just as good and if fruits and vegetables are frozen within hours of picking they can in some cases be even better nutritionally.

The addition of frozen fruit to smoothie bowls gives the most wonderful, almost ice cream-like texture. If your blender is tough enough to crush ice cubes then there is no need to defrost the fruit first, providing the fruit has been frozen diced or left whole if small in the case of strawberries, raspberries, blueberries or blackberries.

Fresh fruit can be expensive and can go soft in the refrigerator before you have a chance to use it all. Don't bin those bananas in the fruit bowl that have brown speckles, just catch them before they go too far. Cut down on waste, save money and make your own freezer packs when the fruits are in season or on special offer, and the nutritional content will not be affected.

HOMEMADE FRUIT FREEZER PACKS

Prepare the fruit as you would if eating immediately, so peel and stone (pit) mangoes and papaya. Cut the peel and core away from pineapple slices and then dice. Hull strawberries, raspberries and blackberries, if needed. Peel and slice ripe bananas. Arrange fruits with the same types together on large baking sheets and open freeze, that is freeze them uncovered for an hour or so until hard. Loosen the fruits then take off the baking sheet and pack into plastic bags. Press out the air, seal and label. Bananas will only freeze for a maximum of 1 month; exotic fruits such as mangoes, papaya and pineapples up to 3 months; and summer berry fruits up to 6 months. Fruits with a high water content will go a little soft after freezing but as they are going to be blitzed in a blender to make a smoothie this is fine.

FRUITY ICE CUBES

Fruit can also be frozen as a purée. Prepare individual fruits as above then blitz in a blender without sugar. Depending on water content, some may need a tablespoon or two of additional water to blend smoothly.

Pour the purée into sections of an ice cube tray. Freeze until firm then turn out and pack each fruit type in different plastic bags. Squeeze out the air then seal and label. Banana purée does not freeze well, so keep as slices only. Each ice cube is about 2 teaspoons of purée. Use as many ice cubes as you need and either defrost at room temperature or microwave briefly until soft. Drizzle over smoothie bowls for a dramatic and eye-catching swirl.

Wholegrains

All wholegrains are rich in complex carbs which are digested slowly by the body, helping to maintain sugar levels in the blood and leave you feeling fuller for longer, while their high fibre content helps to lower blood cholesterol. The risk of heart disease may be up to 30% lower in people who regularly eat wholegrains.

Traditionally oats have been made into porridge-style breakfasts simmered in dairy milk, you can also use nut or soya milk, and sweeten with fruits rather than refined sugars. Buy oats as jumbo, standard sized or porridge (rolled) oats and oatmeal. Oatmeal is the whole grain cut into small pieces and is available as coarse, medium or fine depending on how it is milled. Or try porridge made with a mix of oats, barley and rye flakes.

Muesli sold in the supermarkets is very often sweetened so make up your own grain mixes with porridge oats, rye and barley flakes, adding in a few quinoa flakes for an easy protein boost. Granola is easy to make at home with just a little olive oil or coconut oil and a tablespoon or two of honey or maple syrup, and bakes in under 20 minutes.

Quinoa is one of the few plant foods to contain all essential amino acids making it a complete protein source. Naturally gluten-free, it also contains vitamin B and E, a wide range of minerals and fibre. Quinoa is available in three colours, black, red and the more usual creamy coloured grains, plus flakes which are great added to power balls or smoothies.

Although we think of quinoa as a grain it is actually the seed of the plant. This also applies to buckwheat, tiny triangular seeds from a plant related to rhubarb, sold either as buckwheat groats or as flakes; both make great porridge or a base for a bircher-style breakfast bowl.

Think of wholegrains and we automatically think of rather worthy brown rice, however you can also look out for Thai black rice and the more expensive wild black rice or the nutty tasting red Camargue rice.

If you are following a gluten-free diet there are some grains that you should avoid, namely rye, barley and of course wheat. Oats contain avenin, a protein similar to gluten but may be tolerated by some people with coeliac disease. Check with your health consultant before introducing and always read the nutritional information on the pack for the gluten-free symbol. Some may be contaminated with gluten-containing cereals during harvesting or milling.

Opposite, clockwise from top: buckwheat grains, buckwheat flakes, oatmeal (centre), oats, quinoa and quinoa flakes. Left: black rice.

Nuts and seeds

Adding a few nuts and seeds to a smoothie bowl, layered jar or porridge topping is an easy way to boost protein levels. As they do not contain the whole range of amino acids that the body needs to make protein, combine with other foods such as soya products and grains.

GO NUTTY

Nuts provide most of the B vitamins and the minerals phosphorous, iron, copper and potassium. They are also one of the richest sources of vitamin E, but both vitamin E and thiamine are destroyed when nuts are roasted. Walnuts, peanuts and hazelnuts are especially rich in essential fatty acids which are vital for normal tissue growth and development. Selenium can be a difficult mineral for someone on a vegan diet to obtain and Brazil nuts are an excellent source of selenium; just one nut can give you a day's supply.

Unfortunately the fat content of nuts does bump up the calories but also helps to boost energy, so just eat in moderation. Most varieties contain more than 550 calories per 100g/3¾oz. Chestnuts are the only nut not high in fat. It is much better to add a few nuts to power-boosting snacks or smoothies than to munch on a bowl of nuts as a snack.

Homemade or bought peanut, almond, hazelnut or cashew nut butters are not only delicious spread on to toast but boost protein levels in smoothies too. If you buy, choose brands that do not have added sugar and only the minimum of salt. If adding peanut butter to a smoothie bowl or healthy snack always check before offering to a friend or visitor, in case of peanut allergy. Do not give whole nuts or seeds to children under five and even if older, do so under supervision to avoid any risk of choking.

Left, clockwise from top right: cashew nuts, pecan nuts, walnuts, pistachio nuts, almonds, hazelnuts, Brazil nuts and toasted coconut (which is technically not a nut but a fruit).

SOW THE SEED

Seeds are cheap to buy, easy to pick up in the supermarket and add extra nutritional value to any smoothie or power ball. They make a great protein booster for those who do not eat meat and are high in fibre, although be beware they are high in calories. 1 tablespoon can contain up to 100 calories and this is derived from the unsaturated or good fat that they contain.

Pumpkin seeds contain iron for healthy blood, magnesium for maintaining healthy body cells and zinc for normal growth and development. Sunflower seeds are used to make oil and margarine. They contain useful amounts of vitamin C and are high in linoleic acid needed for the maintenance of cell membranes. Sesame seeds are an essential cooking ingredient in the Middle East where they are blended into tahini and added to hummus. The seeds contain vitamin E and calcium.

Flaxseeds, also called linseeds, can be bought as brown or golden seeds. They are one of the best food sources of lignans, which are rich in antioxidants and act as phytoestrogens which help balance hormone levels. They also contain omega 3 and 6 essential fatty acids, plus magnesium, manganese, vitamin B and fibre. Buy ready ground or grind your own at home so that the body can absorb the vital nutrients that they contain. As these seeds have such tough outer

Above, clockwise from top left: hulled hemp seeds, sunflower seeds, pumpkin seeds, chia seeds, sesame seeds (centre), flaxseeds and ground flaxseeds.

walls, if you leave them whole they will just pass right through the body adding only roughage to the diet.

Chia seeds add protein, fibre, omega 3, 6 and 9 fatty acids plus calcium, iron, copper and zinc. When mixed with liquid they form a gel, so serve any smoothie or dessert with chia seeds as soon as you have made it. Or stir in a little extra liquid just before serving.

Rich in essential fatty acids with two thirds of omega 6 and one third omega 3 fatty acids, hemp contains all 20 amino acids, including the essential ones for boosting protein for those on a vegan diet, as well as B vitamins, vitamin E, carotene, calcium and magnesium. Buy as hulled seeds as these are easier for the body to digest and extract the important nutrients, as oil or as a fine green powder.

Liquid refreshment

All smoothies require additional liquid to the mix of fruit, vegetables, nuts and seeds. You can choose from unsweetened nut, soya, rice and oat milk, canned coconut milk, clear coconut water, fruit juices or water – the choice is very much yours. While certain liquids have been specified in the recipes throughout this book do swap if you prefer.

KEEP HYDRATED

If you don't drink enough you can become tired, have poor concentration and headaches, and may feel light-headed. Drinking plenty of water also helps to prevent constipation, kidney stones and urinary tract infections. Age, gender, build, lifestyle and activity, not to mention the weather, also affect how much we need to drink.

Drinking water is key to staying healthy. Women should aim for at least 1.6 litres/ 2½ pints, men 2 litres/3½ pints of water a day. It sounds a lot but if you keep a glass of water on your desk at work, always have water on the table at meal times and swap some of your daily cups of tea and coffee for water it is achievable. Tea, herb tea and coffee also count, although don't overdo the number that you have, especially cups of strong coffee. Smoothies also aid hydration from the water in fruit and vegetables and added liquids such as nut milks or coconut water.

TAP WATER OR MINERAL WATER?

This is very much personal preference and budget. Tap water is under-rated and free, while bottled water has to be bought from the supermarket and carried home. For those who like really cold water, keep a bottle of tap water in the refrigerator or pour through a water filter and store in the door of the refrigerator, ready and waiting. While manufacturers of mineral water claim the benefits of the natural minerals they contain, the amounts are small and as you are adding this to a smoothie that is packed with nutrient-boosting vegetables and fruit the benefits of the bought bottled water are slightly overshadowed.

DAIRY-FREE MILKS

Over the past few years there has been a huge rise in popularity and availability of nut milks, soya, rice, oat and hemp milks. No longer sold just in specialist health food stores, non-dairy milks are now so popular that they are available in all supermarkets and even smaller corner shops. There is a huge demand but why? More and more people are moving away from a diet rich in red meat and saturated fats to a healthier, cleaner wholegrain diet that is free from not just meat and fish but dairy too. Many people blame dairy milk for feeling bloated or adding to symptoms of indigestion, IBS, sinus problems or skin complaints while others just prefer the taste. A small minority of people do have a serious allergy to the milk sugar lactose and milk protein casein. But if you don't follow a vegan diet do continue to use and enjoy dairy milk, either as semi-skimmed (low-fat) or skimmed, for a natural calcium-boosting, bone-strengthening base to porridge, smoothie bowls or soups.

Read the labels before buying non-dairy milks and choose unsweetened brands that have been fortified with calcium and vitamin D. Some brands will also have added vitamin B12, a vitamin that is difficult to get on a vegan diet. Calorie counts vary slightly and the taste varies too. All dairy-free milks below are suitable for a vegan diet.

Soya milk – this has the strongest taste and contains more protein than the other non-dairy milks; it also contains vitamins A, D and B12 plus potassium. It is usually fortified with calcium.

Almond milk – lower in calories than soya milk, this is more like cow's milk in texture but is slightly beige in colour; it is free from cholesterol, saturated fat and lactose. Even though almonds are a good source of protein, almond milk is not, but does contain vitamins A and D. Buy it fortified with calcium.

Rice milk – this is the least allergenic of all the non-dairy milks. It is high in carbohydrates but contains almost no protein. During processing the natural carbs change to sugars, giving this milk a natural sweetness. Buy fortified with calcium. Rice milk has a thinner texture and doesn't add colour to smoothies.

Oat milk – made simply with oats, water and just a little salt for flavour, this also has a thinner texture and again doesn't add colour to the smoothies that they are stirred into.

Hemp milk – this can be a little grainy but is higher in heart-healthy omega 3 fatty acids than the other milks.

COCONUT MILK OR COCONUT WATER?

Canned coconut milk makes a great store-cupboard standby with a long shelf life. Choose from standard or reduced-fat for a creamy mildly coconut flavour in fruit smoothies. Coconut milk is lactose-free so suitable for those who are lactose intolerant. Decant any coconut milk left

in the can to a plastic container, cover, store in the refrigerator and use within 2 days.

Coconut water is the clear liquid taken from immature coconuts. Buy in cartons in the chiller cabinet alongside the other fruit juices. There are some big claims out there about the benefits of coconut water from anti-ageing to anti-carcinogenic and anti-thrombotic. While they may not all be true, coconut water is naturally low in calories, contains easily digested sugars, and offers five essential electrolyte minerals: calcium, magnesium, phosphorous, potassium and sodium.

Nutrient boosters

Visit the health food shop and you will find a range of unusual nutrient-boosting powders. If you are not familiar with them all, here is a run-down.

Spirulina – this dark blue-green powder (see opposite) is made from dried algae and contains 60% protein, vitamin B12, a difficult vitamin to get for those on a vegan diet, plus essential fatty acids. It is also thought to have immune-boosting properties and may help normalize blood pressure.

Chlorella – this is also a dark green powdered algae, but unlike spirulina has a hard cell wall that needs to be broken down during manufacture so that the body can absorb it during digestion.

Hemp powder – this is another green powder, and like spirulina is packed with protein, in fact it is one of only a few plants to contain all amino acids, as well as being rich in essential fatty acids omega 6 and 3 and a good source of vitamin E. Can also be bought as hemp oil or hulled seeds.

Wheatgrass – this can be bought in powdered form or as grass sold in small trays. As only small amounts are used at a time, powdered wheatgrass makes a handy store-cupboard nutrient booster. Wheatgrass contains all eight essential amino acids needed by the body for growth and repair of all cells, plus B vitamins, vitamins C, E and K, and iron.

Matcha – sold in concentrated powdered form this green tea contains 137 times the amount of antioxidants than the same weight of regular green tea. Buy in small tea bags and soak in boiled water in the same way as making your usual herbal tea.

Moringa – this green powder is derived from the dried leaves of the native Indian moringa tree, also known as the miracle tree, and has long been used in traditional Indian medicine for its anti-bacterial properties and as a digestive aid. Moringa contains all essential amino acids plus it is rich in vitamins A, B, E and the minerals magnesium, potassium and calcium, as well as small amounts of iron.

Acai – these little berries can be found in the Amazon rainforest. The raw fruit is trickier to get in your local supermarket as it goes rancid quickly after picking so buy in tiny teabag-sized sachets of freeze-dried powdered fruit (see left) and sprinkle into smoothies or use as a decoration. Rich in antioxidants, healthy omega fatty acids and fibre, it can also be bought as frozen purée.

TRY TO REDUCE SUGARS

We should all be trying to cut down on the amount of sugar we eat. Top of the list must be to cut down on fizzy drinks, chocolate bars and packaged cereals as these contain very few other health benefits and are often referred to as empty calories. While fruit can be high in sugar, they also contain lots of nutrients that are good for us such as antioxidants, vitamins, minerals and fibre.

Added sugars shouldn't make up more than 5% of the energy or calorie intake that you get from food and drink a-day. That's about 30–35g or 7 tsp a day for anyone aged 11 and older.

• Reduce the amount of sugar that you add to tea and coffee, smoothies or fruit salads. Avoid highly refined white sugars.

• Add banana, strawberries, blueberries or grated apple to porridge instead of sugar.

• Choose unsweetened nut and soya milk and unsweetened peanut butter.

• Pour honey or maple syrup into a teaspoon before drizzling over a smoothie bowl rather than pouring straight from the bottle.

• When making your own smoothie combos add a mix of fruit and vegetables and taste before adding extra sweetener in the form of honey or maple syrup, date honey or agave syrup.

• Reduce the amount of added sugar to muesli bars, brownies and cookies by adding naturally sweet apple purée, grated apple, beetroot or steamed sweet potato.

Baobab – this white powder comes from a dried coconut-sized fruit from Africa. Rich in potassium, calcium, vitamin C, antioxidants and small amounts of iron, it is thought to aid digestion and enhance the growth of probiotic bacteria in the gut.

Raw cacao – this is made by cold pressing unroasted cocoa beans, so removing the fat but retaining important antioxidants, minerals and the amino acid tryptophan which aids relaxation and sleep. The cocoa powder usually used in baking is darker in colour as it has been roasted at high temperatures, so lowering the overall nutritional value and giving it a stronger, slightly bitter taste.

Choosing a smoothie maker

A smoothie maker is really a blender and like all blenders they come with different jug or pitcher styles, motor sizes and price tags. So how do you choose?

There are top-of-the-range powerful blenders (such as Vitamix) that make light work of crushing ice, blitzing soups, making fruit purées, homemade nut butters, grinding seeds, and of course making ultra-smooth smoothies.

The Vitamix model has a large plastic blender goblet and lid that is easy to put together and importantly very easy to wash. Simply add water, a drop of washing up liquid and turn on the machine for easy cleaning. The only downside is that it is tall when the goblet is on the base so will not fit on the work surface under an overhead cupboard. With that powerful motor comes a pretty hefty price tag, but if you like cooking and will use this ultra-durable blender for more than just making smoothies then this could be the machine for you.

Mid-priced blenders look stylish and come in a variety of colours, sleek black, glossy cream or white bases, even bright bold primaries. Blender goblets vary in size and can come in clear or ridged glass or plastic. Choose one that can crush ice so that you know the motor will be tough enough to give you a very smooth smoothie. Some machines may also come with a smoothie-style goblet with a screw top so that you can take your smoothie with you, plus a smaller goblet and different blade fittings for grinding nuts, seeds and coffee beans.

Nutribullet-style blenders are designed for just making individual portion-sized smoothies. Technically not a blender but an extractor these are not much bigger than a water bottle. Easy-to-assemble, easy-to-use and very compact, these will fit on the work surface of even the smallest kitchen. Plus they are quick and easy to wash. Buy one that has several different-sized goblets, plus two different blades, one for grinding nuts and seeds and the second for softer fruits, along with screw-on lids so that you simply add on the

WHAT ABOUT FOOD PROCESSORS?

While food processors can blend smoothies and soups, they don't really blend mixtures of raw beetroot, carrot, apple, small seeds or nuts finely enough, the kind of ingredients that regularly appear in a smoothie blend. They are also big, so generate a lot of washing up for just an individual smoothie. Where they are good though is for blitzing together power ball ingredients, where soft Medjool dates, nuts, seeds and oats are mixed together then rolled into energy-boosting healthy balls.

lid to transport rather than decant into a second container. Some models also sell small insulated bags that just fit the blender goblet for drinks on the go. Always make sure to add liquid; even soft berries will require a splash of water, coconut water or nut milk to blend smooth.

Other models can make a good alternative to a Nutribullet. Choice and budget is up to you. If it is too cheap it probably won't have a powerful enough motor to blend raw carrots, beetroot or whole seeds for a really smooth smoothie, so bear in mind what kind of ingredients you will be adding to your smoothie. If it is mainly avocado, berries, bananas, kale, spinach and ready-ground seeds then a cheaper model will be able to cope, but not harder roots or fine seeds. Also factor in how often you think you will be making a healthy smoothie. If you are new to the idea, then start with a cheaper model and upgrade when you get hooked.

How to make a smoothie bowl

Smoothie bowls are thick fruit or fruit and vegetable mixtures blended until smooth. For ingredients that have a high water content there is no need to add extra liquid (as in this example strawberry and chia smoothie bowl). For others, top up with a little water, apple juice, nut, soya or coconut milk or coconut water.

If your blender isn't very powerful, grind or finely chop the nuts and seeds on their own or make up your favourite mix and store in a plastic container then sprinkle it over the fruit and vegetable smoothie just before blending with liquid. Adding a mix of fresh and frozen fruits will give the finished smoothie an ice cream-like texture.

Don't overfill your blender and always screw the lid on firmly. Begin on a low setting if your machine has variable settings, then gradually increase once the ingredients have been partially blended until they are super-smooth.

For the best taste and the highest nutrient content, serve the smoothie the minute it is made and decorated. Sprinkle in a few nuts such as unblanched almonds, cashew nut pieces or hazelnuts, and a tablespoon or two of fibre-boosting grains such as rolled oats or protein-packed quinoa flakes. Add a teaspoonful or two of ground flaxseeds, hulled hemp seeds, sunflower or pumpkin seeds and complete with a little powdered nutrient-boosting spirulina, wheatgrass or chlorella powder.

Blend until smooth then pour into a bowl. Now the fun can start, unleash the artist in you! Decorate with stripes, rings, dots or swirls of fruit purée, cashew cream or yogurt. Multi-coloured whole or sliced fruits, tiny cauliflower or broccoli florets, a little shredded kale or lettuce, extra ground or whole seeds, or chopped nuts in patterns on top... for an eye-catching start to the day.

STRAWBERRY AND CHIA CRUSH

1 Prepare the fruit, in this case hull the strawberries, chop the lemon and cut the banana into slices.

2 Add the fruit to the blender goblet. For fruit and vegetable mixes with a lower water content, add liquid at this stage.

3 Screw on the lid and blend until smooth. Adjust the consistency if needed with a little water or coconut water. Add the seeds, chia seeds in this case, and mix together.

4 Pour the smoothie into a serving bowl and get all the smoothie mixture out of the blender with a flexible plastic spatula.

5 Decorate and add toppings as you wish. In this case add small spoonfuls of natural yogurt to the top of the smoothie bowl.

6 Run a skewer or small knife through the yogurt for a marbled effect. If you like you can arrange sliced strawberries and sliced banana on top and sprinkle with a few hulled hemp seeds, a few extra chia seeds and a little acai powder before serving straight away.

How to make a layered jar

Arrange the layered breakfasts in glass tumblers if serving at home or pack into clip-top or mason-style jars for a breakfast on the go. Make sure to add a spoon to your bag.

A great way to have a healthy superfood breakfast on the go is to make a jar you can safely carry with you. Layers make it easy to assemble and pretty to look at! Mashed and puréed fruits are layered with finely shredded or sliced ingredients. A base of muesli or granola adds crunch and fibre, while spoonfuls of natural dairy or non-dairy yogurt or cashew nut cream add smoothness and creaminess to these delicious portable breakfasts.

RAINBOW IN A JAR

1 Spoon the base layer ingredients, muesli in this case, into the base of a clip-top or screw-topped jar. Drizzle over the chosen liquid, a little apple juice or water is used here, to moisten.

2 Prepare the next layer, for this recipe coarsely grate the apple and very finely shred the kale. Spoon the apple then the kale into the jar.

3 Prepare the next layer, here coarsely grate the beetroot and spoon over the kale.

4 Prepare the next layer, here we add prepared fresh or frozen mango to a blender goblet with a little water. Screw on the lid and blend until smooth. Spoon the purée over the beetroot.

5 Add the desired toppings, in this case a spoonful of homemade cashew nut cream and a sprinkle of spirulina powder, if liked.

6 Clip or screw the lid in place and take to work or chill in the refrigerator overnight ready for the morning.

GETTING THE BALANCE RIGHT
This layered jar has all the nutrients needed for a healthy diet: vital vitamins and minerals, protein from the oats and cashew nuts, good carbs in the apple, beetroot and muesli, and cholesterol-lowering pectin in the apple and muesli; while the cashew nuts contain a mix of saturated, monounsaturated and polyunsaturated fats in a healthy ratio of 1:2:1.

Basic recipes

We are all strapped for time in the morning so make up a batch of homemade muesli or granola to store in jars, ready and waiting to be dipped into. These are great to layer with fruit purée and yogurt or to sprinkle over smoothie bowls.

MUESLI BASE
Makes 350g/12oz/3½ cups

Making your own muesli takes just minutes and means that you know exactly what is in it. No added sugar or preservatives, just healthy, fibre-boosting grains and seeds for a slow sustained energy-boosting breakfast.

100g/3¾oz/1 cup jumbo rolled oats
75g/3oz/¾ cup barley flakes
75g/3oz /¾ cup rye flakes
50g/2oz/½ cup quinoa flakes
4 tbsp/¼ cup ground flaxseeds
4 tbsp/¼ cup sunflower seeds
4 tbsp/¼ cup pumpkin seeds

1 Add all the ingredients to a bowl and mix together. Spoon into a jar, screw or clip on the lid and store in a cool place for up to 2 weeks.

NUT MUESLI
Makes 275g/10oz/2¼ cups

An ABC of protein-boosting almonds, Brazil nuts and coconut go into this, but do mix and match or add different kinds of nuts if you have them. Scatter over smoothie bowls, layer in glasses with yogurt and puréed fruit, or serve simply with your personal milk choice.

175g/6oz/1½ cups muesli base
15g/½oz/¼ cup desiccated (dry unsweetened shredded) coconut
40g/1½oz/¼ cup Brazil nuts, roughly chopped
40g/1½oz/¼ cup unblanched almonds, roughly chopped

1 Add all the ingredients to a bowl and mix together. Spoon into a jar, screw or clip on the lid and store in a cool place for up to 2 weeks.

MAKE OVER THAT MUESLI
You might also like to stir into a batch or portion of basic muesli…
• Festive ground cinnamon, pecan nuts and dried cranberries
• Tropical ground ginger, coconut flakes, diced dried pineapple and diced dried apricots
• Gorgeous dried goji berries, diced dried mango and roughly chopped unblanched almonds
• Super seedy chia and sesame seeds
• Very finely chopped dried orange and lemon rind for a citrus tang

Left: Energy 442kcal/1859kJ; Protein 15.9g; Carbohydrate 55.4g, of which sugars 0.7g; Fat 18.9g, of which saturates 2.0g; Cholesterol 0mg; Calcium 52mg; Fibre 7.9g; Sodium 31mg (per 100g).
Right: Energy 512kcal/2136kJ; Protein 15.8g; Carbohydrate 37.8g, of which sugars 1.8g; Fat 34.0g, of which saturates 7.5g; Cholesterol 0mg; Calcium 96mg; Fibre 6.3g; Sodium 24mg (per 100g).

HONEYED GRANOLA

Makes 175g/6oz/2 cups

Made with just the minimum amount of oil and honey, this is a crisp crunchy golden granola that is lovely sprinkled over smoothie bowls, served with milk and fruit or just munched on as a healthy snack.

2 tbsp virgin olive oil
2 tbsp clear honey
25g/1oz/¼ cup rolled oats
25g/1oz/¼ cup quinoa flakes
40g/1½oz/¼ cup unblanched hazelnuts,
   roughly chopped
2 tbsp sunflower seeds
2 tbsp sesame seeds

1 Preheat the oven to 180°C/350°F/Gas 4. Line a large baking sheet with baking parchment.
2 Warm the oil and honey together in a medium pan then take off the heat and stir in the oats, quinoa flakes, hazelnuts and seeds.
3 Tip the mixture out on to the lined sheet.
4 Spread the granola out into an even layer. Bake for 8–10 minutes until crisp and golden around the edges.
5 The granola will cook more quickly around the edges so stir the browner edges into the centre, spread into an even layer once more and return to the oven for 5–10 minutes until evenly golden brown all over.
6 Stir once more to loosen from the paper then leave to cool and harden. Spoon the granola into a plastic container or jar, seal and keep in the refrigerator for up to 1 week.

Energy 627kcal/2611kJ; Protein 13.4g; Carbohydrate 38.6g, of which sugars 14.4g; Fat 47.7g, of which saturates 5.8g; Cholesterol 0mg; Calcium 182mg; Fibre 7.8g; Sodium 17mg (per 100g).

FRUITY CACAO GRANOLA

Makes 300g/11oz/2¾ cups

Just because you are trying to eat in a healthier way doesn't mean that chocolate-flavoured cereal is off the menu. Antioxidant-boosting cacao rather than sweetened roasted cocoa has been added to this mixed grain granola. Sweetness is added with the Middle Eastern date honey. Sprinkle over smoothie bowls, layer in glasses with fruit purées or spoon into bowls and top with milk of your choice.

2 tbsp virgin olive oil
2 tbsp date honey
2 tbsp orange juice
50g/2oz/½ cup jumbo rolled oats
50g/2oz/½ cup rye flakes
50g/2oz/½ cup barley flakes
1 tbsp cacao powder
3 tbsp dried cranberries
2 tbsp dried goji berries
65g/2½oz/10 dried apricots, diced

1 Preheat the oven to 180°C/350°F/Gas 4. Line a large baking sheet with baking parchment.
2 Warm the oil, date honey and orange juice in a medium pan. Take off the heat and stir in the oats, rye and barley flakes.
3 Tip out on to the lined sheet and spread in an even layer. Bake for 8–10 minutes then stir, so that the browner crisper edges are moved to the centre. Cook for 2–5 minutes more until evenly browned.
4 Sift over the cacao powder and sprinkle over dried fruit, stir together to loosen the granola from the paper, then leave to cool.
5 Pack into a jar and keep in the refrigerator for up to 1 week.

COOK'S TIP As date honey is made with dates rather than taken from a hive it is suitable for those following a vegan diet. But if this doesn't apply then ordinary honey could be used instead.

Energy 332kcal/1403kJ; Protein 24.9g; Carbohydrate 55.3g, of which sugars 23.9g; Fat 10.8g, of which saturates 4.4g; Cholesterol 0mg; Calcium 57mg; Fibre 4.9g; Sodium 55mg (per 100g).

HOMEMADE ALMOND OR CASHEW MILK

Nut, oat, soya and rice milks are now readily available in the supermarket, either chilled or longlife. If you would like to try to make your own at home, almond or cashew nut milks are the simplest to try.

1 Roughly chop 125g/4½oz/1 cup unblanched almonds (the ones with the brown skins) or the same weight of cashew nut pieces and add to a large plastic container. Cover with 1 litre/ 1¾ pints/4 cups cold filtered water. Add the lid to the container and leave to soak overnight in the refrigerator or a cool place.

2 Transfer small batches of the almonds or cashew nuts and water to a blender, screw on the lid and blend until smooth. Strain the nut purée through a fine sieve or strainer lined with muslin or cheesecloth. You should have 1 litre/1¾ pints/4 cups of nut milk. Transfer to a bottle, seal and keep in the refrigerator for up to 2 days. If it separates, simply stir it before use.

3 The remaining nut meal in the sieve or strainer can be kept and a tablespoon or two added to smoothie bowls, stirred into yogurt or mixed into soups before blending.

CASHEW CREAM

Makes 250g/9oz/1 generous cup

Homemade cashew cream makes a great vegan alternative to whipped dairy cream. It is delicious spooned over smoothie bowls or soups and homemade cakes too. Look out for cashew nut pieces in the health food store or supermarket as they are much cheaper than the whole nuts.

150g/5oz/1 cup cashew nut pieces
Few drops vanilla extract
2 tsp maple syrup or sweetener of choice

1 Add the cashews to a bowl and pour over cold water to generously cover the nuts, then cover the bowl with a plate and chill in the refrigerator or a cool place overnight. Drain the nuts in a colander, reserving the water.

2 Add the nuts and 4 tbsp of the soaking water to a blender goblet. Screw on the lid and blitz until smooth. You may need to scrape down the sides of the blender goblet once or twice and if very thick add in a little extra soaking water to get a really smooth cream. Add the vanilla and sweetener and blend briefly together.

3 Spoon into a jar, smooth the surface then screw or clip on the lid. Chill in the refrigerator for up to 3 days.

COOK'S TIP If you have a vanilla pod or bean use this in place of bottled vanilla extract. Slit the pod lengthways then scrape out the black seeds with a knife and add to the cashew cream. Don't throw the scraped pod away but get the very last vanilla flavour out by adding to fruit and water when making a fruit compote or when cooking porridge. Discard the pod before serving.

Healthy eating plan

Starting the day with a smoothie bowl or hot energy-boosting breakfast is an easy way to begin a new healthy eating regime for all the family. Research proves that children that eat a good breakfast concentrate better at school; for adults too, if you haven't had breakfast it can be hard to make those tricky decisions at work.

For a healthy diet to succeed it needs to be achievable, and by starting with a nutritional breakfast you will feel energized and able to cope with whatever the day throws at you. A small change such as what you eat for breakfast can snowball into bigger changes as you begin to modify and introduce healthier foods to other meals too.

For our main meal of the day, health professionals advise that one third of our plate should be filled with vegetables, but this doesn't mean that they need to be kept separate. Add extra veggies to casseroles, or as purée in tomato sauces to go with pasta so that the family don't realise that they are there. Add carrots, celeriac or swede (rutabaga) to mashed potato. (Unfortunately,

potatoes don't count as one of our five-a-day of vegetables or fruit.)

Unless you are vegetarian try to reduce the amount of meat that you eat, include fish twice a week and make one of those an oily fish. Aim for two meat-free suppers a week to boost your vegetable consumption even more.

Keep biscuits, cookies and cake as a treat and cut out the fizzy drinks. Refined sugar is the bad guy on the block. Yes there is sugar in fruit, even in some vegetables such as beetroot or parsnips, but their sugar comes with additional health-boosting vitamins and minerals, unlike the sugar that is found in a fizzy drink which has no healthy qualities at all. Opt for snacks with natural fruit sugars and wholegrains for slow-release energy.

Junk food, irregular meals, not to mention lack of sleep will leave you feeling tired, irritable and stressed. The old adage that your body is a temple may seem comical but we will only feel as well as the food that we put in. Eat regularly to keep your body full of energy and on top form.

The plan here is a sample menu for a balanced weekly diet but of course you should adapt recipe suggestions for yourself, for instance if you are vegetarian, vegan or gluten-free.

7 day planner

SATURDAY

Breakfast Multi-grain banana berry bowl, p40.
Lunch Grilled bacon sandwiches on brown bread.
Snack Chocolate popcorn bars, p128.
Supper Thai green curry with mixed prawns (shrimp) and salmon plus lots of mixed vegetables.

SUNDAY

Breakfast Broccoli and avocado wake-up bowl, p116.
Lunch Smoked mackerel salad with hard-boiled egg wedges, tomatoes, cucumber, mixed leaves and a horseradish-flavoured yogurt dressing.
Snack Chocolate popcorn bars, p128.
Supper Roast chicken, roast potatoes, carrots and parsnips, steamed green vegetables.

MONDAY

Breakfast Bircher muesli pots, p74.
Lunch Baked potato topped with tuna mashed with a little low-fat cream cheese and topped with salad.
Snack Energy chocolate bark, p130.
Supper Stir-fry pack mixed vegetables tossed with any remaining cold roast chicken, thin shreds of omelette and served with egg noodles.

TUESDAY

Breakfast Bircher muesli pots, p74.
Lunch Cheese and salad sandwich with brown bread.
Snack Flapjack cookies with ginger and turmeric, p126.
Supper Shepherd's pie made with lean minced (ground) beef or minced turkey, carrots and mushrooms and topped with mashed potato and swede (rutabaga). Serve with frozen peas.

WEDNESDAY

Breakfast Spinach and spirulina smoothie bowl, p102.
Lunch Hummus, warm pitta bread and tomato salad.
Snack Flapjack cookies with ginger and turmeric, p126.
Supper Chunky mixed vegetable soup with tomatoes, kale, can of mixed beans, (bell) peppers and smoked paprika. Serve with warm crusty bread.

THURSDAY

Breakfast Strawberry and chia crush bowl, p110.
Lunch Baked beans on whole-wheat toast.
Snack Sweet potato brownie bars, p134.
Supper Butternut squash and sage risotto with parmesan.

FRIDAY

Breakfast Very berry oatmeal, p42.
Lunch Couscous salad with chopped herbs, tomatoes, prawns and a lemon and olive oil dressing.
Snack Prune double deckers, p142.
Supper Tagliatelle with turkey meatballs and homemade garlicky tomato sauce.

Detox do's and don'ts

Going on a detox diet is the perfect way to give your digestive system a break. We bombard our body with additives, preservatives, refined sugar and carbs not to mention red meat and full-fat dairy foods. A detox is a way of giving your digestive system a break. This is not a diet to do in the long term but for a few weeks only; think of it as a foodie holiday.

We have all felt at some time or another that we just want a break, whether we have overdone things over the Christmas holiday period, eaten far too much rich food on that long summer break or just feel fed up with the same old meals. It's not just food, do you rely on a strong coffee to keep you going? It's easy to get into a rut of a daily glass of wine because you have had a stressful day, which then becomes two and by the end of the week your alcohol units are far higher than they should be.

Adding a healthy smoothie bowl, warming wholegrain energy-boosting breakfast, hot fruit soup or layered soya yogurt breakfast is the perfect way to start the day. A good detox diet is based around wholegrains, vegetables and fruit.

Use dairy-free milks and yogurt and give wheat, coffee and booze a miss. Avoid pills, enemas, fasting or 24/7 juicing. Choose instead natural unprocessed ingredients, eat a broad range of foods and up the amount of water that you drink. The clean eating approach is the way to go.

As you are cutting out saturated fats from cheese, dairy and meat you will also find that you may not only feel better but may lose weight or kick-start a diet that has plateaued.

If you have a medical condition do not go on a detox diet without first consulting your medical practitioner, especially if you have diabetes, as a major change in diet could lead to low blood sugar. For everyone else embrace a detox diet that is packed with nutrient-dense vegetables, fruit, nuts, seeds and wholegrains to get you back on track for a healthier eating regime.

7 day planner

SATURDAY

Breakfast Black rice and papaya bowl, p42.
Lunch Baked potato topped with grilled balsamic tomatoes and sprinkled with basil.
Healthy snack Blueberry and coconut wedges, p138.
Supper Roasted butternut squash with smoked paprika and garlic, mixed with a can of green lentils and topped with maple-glazed pecan nuts and baby spinach leaves.

SUNDAY

Breakfast Traffic light layers, p76.
Lunch Lentil dahl with fried onions and spinach.
Healthy snack Energy chocolate bark p 130.
Supper Thai-style green coconut curry with mixed vegetables, tofu and rice noodles.

MONDAY

Breakfast Rainbow in a jar, p84.
Lunch Falafel with cucumber and tomato salad.
Healthy snack Fig and orange power balls, p124.
Supper Roasted sliced aubergine (eggplant) topped with minted parsley and lemon

yogurt and topped with toasted sesame seeds and sprouting seeds. Serve with herby couscous mixed with a bag of spinach, watercress and rocket (arugula) salad and a little lemon and olive oil dressing.

TUESDAY

Breakfast Gingered buckwheat and peach bowl, p48.
Lunch Grated carrot, sprouted seed and chickpea salad.
Healthy snack Flapjack cookies with ginger and turmeric, p126.
Supper Warm quinoa salad topped with roasted (bell) peppers, courgettes (zucchini) and basil.

WEDNESDAY

Breakfast Bowl of cherryaid p96.
Lunch Mixed kale, black rice and blueberry salad with lemon dressing.

Healthy snack Flapjack cookies with ginger and turmeric, p126.
Supper Baked sweet potato wedges served with chickpea, red pepper and tomato chilli.

THURSDAY

Breakfast Beetroot and orange quinoa bowl, p44.
Lunch Root vegetable soup with turmeric and fennel.
Healthy snack Gingered apricot truffle balls, p132.
Supper Stuffed peppers with salad.

FRIDAY

Breakfast Broccoli and apple soup, p60.
Lunch Mixed bean salad with tomatoes, spinach and a chilli tomato dressing.
Healthy snack Gingered apricot truffle balls, p132.
Supper Cauliflower, potato and spinach curry with pilau rice and cucumber raita.

ENERGY-BOOSTING BOWLS

Porridge-style breakfasts get a trendy makeover with mixed grains, nut milks, quinoa, ruby red berries and even beetroot. The oats and other wholegrains help to superpower you through the morning with their slow-released energy, while the combination of fibre, vitamins and minerals they contain has been linked to long term health.

Multi-grain banana berry bowl

SERVES 1

40g/1½oz/⅓ cup multi-grain mix, see below

250ml/8 fl oz/1 cup unsweetened soy milk or dairy milk

For the topping

1 small banana, 100g/3¾oz peeled weight, sliced

2 tsp dried cranberries

15g/½oz/10 blueberries

4 pecan nuts

Few pumpkin seeds

Make up a jar of the multi-grain mix to keep handy, and have sliced bananas and blueberries in the freezer ready and waiting so that you can rustle up this warming and super-satisfying breakfast in no time.

1 Add the multi-grain mix and milk to a small pan and bring the milk just to the boil, then reduce the heat and simmer for about 5 minutes, stirring from time to time until the grains are soft and have absorbed most of the liquid. Add a little extra milk or water, if needed, to get the consistency that you like.

2 Mash half the banana and stir into the porridge then spoon into a serving bowl. Arrange the remaining banana slices down the centre of the bowl, then add a thin line of cranberries down each side, the blueberries, then the nuts and seeds. Serve immediately.

NUTRIENT NOTE While soya, nut and oat milks have risen hugely in popularity, don't forget about dairy milk too. The calcium in milk is easily absorbed by the body and needed for strong bones and teeth. It is added to non-dairy milk. Skimmed dairy milk contains half the calories of whole milk – as most of the fat is removed in skimmed milk it contains slightly higher amounts of water-soluble B vitamins and minerals but slightly less fat-soluble vitamin A.

MULTI-GRAIN MIX
(Makes 200g/7oz or 5 portions)
Add 50g/2oz/½ cup each of rolled oats, barley flakes and rye flakes and 50g/2oz/generous ½ cup quinoa flakes to a bowl and stir together, then spoon into a screw-topped jar and store.

Energy 534kcal/2241kJ; Protein 14.7g; Carbohydrate 67.4g, of which sugars 34.2g; Fat 24.7g, of which saturates 2.1g; Cholesterol 0mg; Calcium 89mg; Fibre 8.7g; Sodium 97mg.

Black rice and papaya bowl

Originally grown just for Chinese emperors and known as 'forbidden rice', black rice is growing in availability and popularity. It contains anthocyanin antioxidants, which are also found in blueberries and give both their dark colour. Cooked with coconut milk and topped with fresh-tasting papaya, this makes a filling and sustaining breakfast that also helps to maintain healthy cholesterol levels, boost minerals and fibre, and detox the body.

1 Add the water and kafir lime leaf, if using, to a medium pan and bring up to the boil. Stir in the rice then lower the heat and simmer uncovered for 20 minutes. Stir in the coconut milk and sweetener and cook for 5–10 minutes, stirring until soft.

2 Spoon the rice into a serving bowl. Mix the papaya with the lime juice, spoon on top of the rice then add the kiwi wedges. Sprinkle with the lime zest, and serve.

SERVES 1

600ml/1 pint/2½ cups water
1 kafir lime leaf, optional
75g/3oz/scant ½ cup black rice rinsed with cold water, drained
75g/3oz/⅓ cup reduced-fat canned coconut milk
2 tsp date syrup or sweetener of choice

For the topping
¼ small papaya, deseeded, peeled or 50g/2oz prepared fruit, mashed
¼ lime, juice and grated zest
½ kiwi, peeled, cut into wedges

COOK'S TIP As black rice takes a while to cook you may like to make this up the night before and even make up double quantities. Store in the refrigerator and then reheat next morning in a small pan or in the microwave, adding a little extra boiling water to loosen the rice again.

Energy 309kcal/1296kJ; Protein 6.2g; Carbohydrate 72.2g, of which sugars 7.3g; Fat 0.7g, of which saturates 0.1g; Cholesterol 0mg; Calcium 52mg; Fibre 1g; Sodium 90mg.

Beetroot and orange quinoa bowl

SERVES 1

40g/1½oz/¼ cup quinoa

1 small beetroot, trimmed weight about 75g/3oz, peeled and coarsely grated

1 red-skinned dessert apple, cored and half coarsely grated

250ml/8fl oz/1 cup water

Juice ½ orange

For the topping

40g/1½oz/¼ cup cashew nut pieces

3 tbsp unsweetened almond milk

1 thin slice root ginger

½ orange, cut into segments

Few pomegranate seeds

Large pinch wheatgrass or spirulina powder, optional

Porridge with a modern twist. Quinoa is one of the few grains to contain all essential amino acids, the building blocks that make up protein. Plus it is cholesterol-free, rich in fibre and minerals and lower in carbs than most grains.

1 Add the quinoa, beetroot and the grated apple to a pan. Pour over the water, bring to the boil then cover and simmer for 10–15 minutes until the quinoa is soft.

2 Meanwhile add the cashew nut pieces, almond milk and root ginger to a blender goblet, screw on the lid and blend to a coarse purée. Spoon into a bowl and rinse the blender goblet.

3 Tip the beetroot mix into a blender goblet, add the orange juice and blend until smooth. Stir in a little extra boiling water if needed to get the consistency that you like. Spoon into a bowl.

4 Spoon the ginger cream on top. Cut the remaining ungrated half of the apple into small pieces and place with the orange over the beetroot smoothie. Sprinkle with the pomegranate seeds and wheatgrass or spirulina, if using, and serve.

COOK'S TIP If you don't have any pomegranate seeds then top the smoothie bowl with a few halved grapes or blueberries.

Energy 450kcal/1887kJ; Protein 15.1g; Carbohydrate 51.4g, of which sugars 25.7g; Fat 21.9g, of which saturates 4g; Cholesterol 0mg; Calcium 93mg; Fibre 6.6g; Sodium 117mg.

Very berry oatmeal

This might send porridge purists running to the Scottish hills but this more modern vibrant-coloured version adds vitamin C boosting berries along with protein, minerals, and vitamin E and B fortifying seeds.

1 Add the oatmeal and water to a small pan, bring to the boil, then simmer gently for 15–20 minutes, stirring until the oatmeal is tender and almost all the liquid has been absorbed.

2 Add the beetroot, kale, frozen berries and coconut milk to a blender goblet. Screw on the lid and blitz until smooth. Stir into the oatmeal and warm through.

3 Pour into a bowl and top with the extra berries, whole and ground seeds and a few coconut shavings.

OATMEAL V PORRIDGE OATS Oatmeal is the whole oat groat or grain that is cut either with metal blades or in Scotland by stones; sometimes call pinhead oatmeal it can be bought in different grades, coarse, medium or fine. Rolled oats are steamed then rolled flat, quick-cook oats have just been steamed for longer before rolling. Both are rich in fibre which can help to lower cholesterol plus contain protein, B vitamins, vitamin E, calcium, iron and potassium.

SERVES 1

25g/1oz/scant ¼ cup medium oatmeal

250ml/8fl oz/1 cup water

75g/3oz/1 small trimmed beetroot, peeled and diced

15g/½oz/½ cup shredded kale

50g/2oz/½ cup fresh or frozen raspberries

50g/2oz/½ cup fresh or frozen blackberries

100g/3½oz/scant ½ cup reduced-fat canned coconut milk

For the topping

50g/2oz mixed berries, defrosted if frozen

2 tsp pumpkin seeds

1 tsp sunflower seeds

1 tsp ground flaxseeds

Few toasted coconut shavings

Energy 260kcal/1100kJ; Protein 10g; Carbohydrate 38g, of which sugars 17.6g; Fat 8.7g, of which saturates 1.2g; Cholesterol 0mg; Calcium 127mg; Fibre 11g; Sodium 180mg.

Gingered buckwheat and peach bowl

Full of protein, vitamins, minerals and good carbs for a slow sustained energy release, this power-packed energizing breakfast will get you racing from the starting blocks.

1 Add the buckwheat and dried apricots to a pan, pour in the water and bring to the boil. Boil for 5 minutes until the groats are softened, stirring from time to time.

2 Transfer the buckwheat, apricots and cooking water to a blender goblet, and add 3 tbsp almond milk, ginger, carrot and half the peach slices. Screw on the lid and blend until smooth. Add extra almond milk if needed to get the consistency that you like.

3 Spoon into a bowl and top with the remaining peach and medjool date slices then sprinkle with the pomegranate seeds and pistachio nuts and serve while hot.

SERVES 1

50g/2oz/¼ cup buckwheat groats, rinsed several times with cold water and drained well

40g/1½oz/6 dried apricots, diced

250ml/8fl oz/1 cup water

3–6 tbsp unsweetened almond milk

1 thin slice root ginger

75g/3oz/1 small carrot, diced

1 small peach, stoned (pitted) and sliced

For the topping

1 medjool date, stoned and sliced

Few pomegranate seeds

Few roughly chopped pistachio nuts

NUTRIENT NOTE Buckwheat is not part of the wheat or grain family at all but are tiny triangular seeds from a plant related to rhubarb. First grown some 4,000 years BC in the Balkans, Asia and the Middle East, buckwheat is rich in soluble fibre and contains magnesium which helps to relax the blood vessels, and to improve blood flow and nutrient delivery while lowering blood pressure. It also contains smaller amounts of manganese, copper and phosphorous and the flavonoid 'rutin' which aids the action of vitamin C and works as an antioxidant.

COOK'S TIP 30g/1oz/¼ cup buckwheat flakes can also be used in place of the whole seeds; these cook quicker in just 4–5 minutes and get very thick, so stir constantly.

Energy 333kcal/1410kJ; Protein 9.5g; Carbohydrate 65.9g, of which sugars 29.2g; Fat 5.3g, of which saturates 0.1g; Cholesterol 0mg; Calcium 88mg; Fibre 12.4g; Sodium 88mg.

Gingered edamame and kale bowl

SERVES 1

50g/2oz/⅓ cup frozen edamame beans, plus a few extra for topping, defrosted

250ml/8fl oz/1 cup boiling water

1 tsp brown rice miso paste

1 slice root ginger

15g/½oz/½ cup shredded kale

25g/1oz or 2 small broccoli florets

½ dessert apple, cored but not peeled, diced

Few fresh coriander (cilantro) leaves, plus extra to decorate

Juice ¼ lime, to taste

For the topping

1 tbsp sprouting mixed beans

2 sugar snap peas, sliced

1 asparagus tip, pared into strips with a vegetable peeler

1 tsp hulled hemp seeds

½ tsp sesame oil

A protein-boosting warm bowl flavoured with miso, ginger and lime for just a hint of the Far East.

1 Add the edamame beans, boiling water, miso and ginger to a pan and simmer for 3 minutes until piping hot. Add to a blender goblet with the kale, broccoli, apple and coriander, screw on the lid and blend until smooth. Adjust with a little extra boiling water, if needed, and add lime juice to taste.

2 Pour into a bowl and sprinkle with a few extra coriander leaves and edamame beans, the sprouting beans, sugar snap peas, asparagus and hemp seeds. Drizzle with the sesame oil and serve.

NUTRIENT NOTE Edamame beans are very young soya beans, frozen while still tiny and bright green; they contain all essential amino acids, making them a handy protein-packed freezer standby that's rich in fibre too. Just half a cup of edamame beans has the same amount of fibre as 4 slices of whole-wheat bread. It is thought that soya may help to reduce LDL or bad cholesterol and raise HDL or good cholesterol, so helping to guard against heart disease.

Energy 139kcal/582kJ; Protein 9.8g; Carbohydrate 9.2g, of which sugars 5.9g; Fat 7.2g, of which saturates 0.9g; Cholesterol 0mg; Calcium 77mg; Fibre 8.4g; Sodium 25mg.

Citrus barley porridge bowl

SERVES 1

25g/1oz barley flakes

½ small orange, finely chopped including flesh, pith and zest

250ml/8fl oz/1 cup water

½ small pear, quartered, cored, no need to peel

90ml/3fl oz/⅓ cup unsweetened almond milk

For the topping

5 blackberries, defrosted if frozen, and halved

4 roughly chopped almonds

1 small piece of dried mango, chopped, optional

1 tsp maple syrup, optional

Adding the whole orange – peel, pith and flesh – adds a wonderful citrusy tang to this warming breakfast, while also boosting fibre levels and tinting the barley porridge a delicate orange.

1 Add the barley flakes, chopped orange and water to a small pan. Bring to the boil then cover and simmer for 10 minutes until the orange is soft, stirring from time to time and more frequently towards the end of cooking as the barley absorbs the water. Top up with a little extra water, if needed, so that the barley doesn't stick to the pan and you get the consistency that you like.

2 Spoon the barley mixture into a blender goblet. Dice half the pear and add to the barley with the almond milk and blend until smooth.

3 Spoon into a mug or bowl and top with the blackberries, almonds, mango if using and a drizzle of maple syrup, if using. Serve immediately.

COOK'S TIP If you cannot eat grains with gluten but can tolerate oats then add these instead of the barley.

Energy 233kcal/980kJ; Protein 6.7g; Carbohydrate 34.1g, of which sugars 15.7g; Fat 8.7g, of which saturates 0.4g; Cholesterol 0mg; Calcium 84mg; Fibre 6.7g; Sodium 75mg.

Red lentil dahl with crispy spiced kale and cauliflower

While dahl may not sound like an obvious choice for breakfast, this light turmeric-spiced version tastes delicious topped with cool soothing natural yogurt and stir-fried kale and cauliflower. An easy way to add 2 of your 5 portions of vegetables in one hit.

1 Add the lentils, turmeric, ginger, carrot and water to a pan and bring the water to the boil. Cover and simmer for about 15 minutes until the lentils are soft. Mash the lentil mixture or mix in a blender if preferred. Add a little salt to taste.

2 Heat the oil in a frying pan, add the cauliflower and kale then sprinkle with the turmeric and cumin and stir-fry for 3–4 minutes until the cauliflower is lightly browned and the kale crisp around the edges.

3 Spoon the dahl into a bowl, spoon the yogurt into the centre and top with the cauliflower, kale and sunflower seeds.

NUTRIENT NOTE Bright yellow turmeric contains curcumin, a substance with powerful anti-inflammatory and antioxidant properties. Used for thousands of years in Chinese and Indian medicine, it is thought it may help with arthritis, inflammatory skin infections and may even help with Alzheimer's and dementia, but more research needs to be done on this.

COOK'S TIP The dahl base could be made the night before, cooled and kept in the refrigerator overnight, so you can just warm it up in the microwave and cook the cauliflower and kale topping just before serving.

SERVES 1

40g/1½oz/¼ cup red lentils

¼ tsp turmeric

1 slice root ginger, finely chopped

75g/3oz/1 small carrot, scrubbed and diced, or golden beetroot

350ml/12fl oz/1½ cups water

Pinch of salt

For the topping

1 tsp olive oil

75g/3oz/4 large pieces cauliflower, cut into tiny florets

25g/1oz/1 cup shredded kale

Large pinch turmeric

Large pinch ground cumin

2 tbsp fat-free natural yogurt or dairy-free alternative

1 tsp sunflower seeds

Energy 234kcal/987kJ; Protein 13.5g; Carbohydrate 32.6g, of which sugars 9.6g; Fat 6.4g, of which saturates 1g; Cholesterol 0mg; Calcium 98mg; Fibre 6g; Sodium 57mg.

FRUIT AND VEGETABLE SOUPS

Quick and easy to make, these fresh-tasting and warming soups are made with a base of nut milks, green tea or water, which is mixed with vibrant nutrient-packed vegetables such as kale and spinach, carrots, corn and peppers. Then they are blended with fruit such as apples, grapes, mango and berries for natural sweetness. A range of toppings including goji berries, dried cranberries, nuts, seeds and tiny broccoli and cauliflower florets are then added, for nutrients and visual appeal!

Pea and avocado soup

SERVES 1

75g/3oz/½ cup frozen peas

250ml/8fl oz/1 cup unsweetened almond milk

½ ripe medium avocado, stoned (pitted), peeled and diced

10g/¼oz/½ cup pea shoots

1 stem fresh mint

For the topping

40g/1½ oz/scant ¼ cup green seedless grapes, halved

2 cauliflower florets, cut into small pieces

Few dried cranberries

½ tbsp roughly chopped unblanched almonds

1 tsp hemp oil

Few tiny mint leaves

Picked and frozen within hours, the humble frozen pea makes a fibre-, thiamine- and vitamin C-boosting base for this creamy velvety-smooth soup.

1 Add the peas and unsweetened almond milk to a small pan and bring to the boil, then simmer for 3 minutes until the peas are hot.

2 Reserve a small amount of avocado and a few pea shoots for decoration and add the rest to a blender goblet with the hot peas and almond milk and the mint. Screw on the lid and blitz until smooth.

3 Pour into a bowl, arrange the grapes and cauliflower in two circles on top then add the remaining avocado and pea shoots to the centre. Add the cranberries and almonds then drizzle with the hemp oil and finish with a few tiny mint leaves.

NUTRIENT NOTE Avocados are thought to be one of the most nutritionally complete fruits, rich in concentrated energy in the form of good monounsaturated fats, plus vitamin B6 which aids energy release; they are also full of powerful antioxidants, with more potassium than a banana.

COOK'S TIP Pea shoots are most often sold in the supermarkets in the summer months; when out of season add the same amount of baby spinach leaves.

Energy 272kcal/1130kJ; Protein 9g; Carbohydrate 16.2g, of which sugars 10g; Fat 19.4g, of which saturates 3.2g; Cholesterol 0mg; Calcium 70mg; Fibre 8.8g; Sodium 11mg.

Broccoli and apple soup

SERVES 1

75g/3oz/1 cup broccoli florets

1 dessert apple, quartered, cored and diced

50g/2oz/¼ cup seedless green grapes

15g/½oz/½ cup baby spinach leaves

2 tbsp reduced-fat canned coconut milk

250ml/8fl oz/1 cup water

For the topping

1 tbsp fat-free natural yogurt or dairy-free alternative

Few coconut flakes

Large pinch spirulina powder

Broccoli is often hailed as a superfood as it is rich in two powerful phytochemicals, indoles and sulforaphane, thought to help boost enzymes that fight cancer-causing agents. It is also rich in the antioxidant vitamins beta-carotene and vitamin C, plus folic acid, vitamin K, iron and potassium, not to mention fibre.

1 Reserve a broccoli floret, a quarter of the apple and a couple of grapes for decoration. Add the rest of the broccoli, apple and grapes to a blender goblet then add the spinach, coconut milk and water. Screw on the lid and blitz until smooth. Pour into a medium pan and warm through.

2 Pour into a big mug or bowl. Spoon the yogurt into the centre. Dice the remaining apple and arrange on the soup with the reserved broccoli cut into small pieces, and halved reserved grapes. Sprinkle with the coconut flakes and spirulina powder and serve.

NUTRIENT NOTE Dark green spirulina powder is made from dried algae and contains 60% protein and essential fatty acids, plus useful amounts of vitamin B12.

Energy 97kcal/409kJ; Protein 4.3g; Carbohydrate 18.7g, of which sugars 18.4g; Fat 1g, of which saturates 0.2g; Cholesterol 0mg; Calcium 85mg; Fibre 5.1g; Sodium 63mg.

Blueberry and blackberry soup with vanilla yogurt

Superfood blueberries and blackberries are just bursting with antioxidants called flavonoids that may help to protect the body from premature ageing, heart disease and degenerative diseases. Some researchers believe that the antioxidant power of blueberries may even help stabilize brain function and protect the neural tissue from oxidative stress, so helping with memory and depression.

1 Add the blackberries, blueberries and coconut milk to a small pan and warm through, or microwave in a bowl if preferred.

2 Add the warm berries and juice to a blender goblet then add the kale. Reserve a few cashew nut pieces for decoration and add the rest to the blender then screw on the lid and blitz until smooth. Pour into a bowl.

3 Stir the vanilla into the yogurt, spoon on to the soup and top with sliced banana, extra blackberries and blueberries, reserved cashew nut pieces, hemp seeds and goji berries.

NUTRIENT NOTE Berries and kale are also rich in fibre, which is essential for the body to aid digestion and to help lower cholesterol. The Department of Health suggests we should all be eating at least 40% more fibre or 5g a day more to take us up to the recommended 18g a day. Although fibre is not digested it nourishes the bacteria in the large bowel and slows the absorption of glucose in the small intestine, so that energy is released gradually and avoids the sugar highs and lows that cause mood swings.

SERVES 1

50g/2oz/½ cup blackberries, plus a few extra for topping

50g/2oz/generous ⅓ cup blueberries, plus a few extra for topping

125ml/4fl oz/½ cup reduced-fat canned coconut milk

25g/1oz/1 cup shredded kale

25g/1oz cashew nut pieces

For the topping

Few drops vanilla extract

2 tbsp fat-free Greek (US strained plain) yogurt or dairy-free alternative

50g/2oz/½ small banana, sliced

1 tsp hulled hemp seeds

1 tsp dried goji berries

Energy 379kcal/1315kJ; Protein 10.4g; Carbohydrate 37g, of which sugars 30.4g; Fat 16.4g, of which saturates 1.7g; Cholesterol 0mg; Calcium 201mg; Fibre 6.8g; Sodium 182mg.

Gingered carrot and mango soup

SERVES 1

75g/3oz or 1 small carrot, scrubbed and sliced

1 thin slice root ginger, no need to peel, quartered

100g/3¾oz/generous ½ cup diced mango, defrost if using frozen

1 tsp baobab powder

125ml/4fl oz/½ cup unsweetened almond milk

For the topping

Few mango slices

1 thin slice root ginger, peeled, cut into thin strips

5 raspberries

4 unblanched almonds, sliced

1 tsp dried goji berries

½ tsp chia seeds

COOK'S TIP Almond milk has been used here but you can add your favourite non-dairy milk. Rice or soya milk would also work well.
NUTRIENT NOTE A diet rich in carotenoids – the pigment that makes food orange – may help lower the risk of heart disease and help protect against cancer. Carrots also help to maintain good eye health and the ability to adjust quickly to changes in light. In traditional medicine, carrots are used for their detoxifying properties.

A pretty pastel orange soup with just a hint of peppery ginger; don't be tempted to be too generous with the ginger or you may overpower the delicate flavour of the creamy smooth mango. Blend together then add a little more at the end if you want to.

1 Add the carrot, ginger, mango and baobab to a blender goblet. Heat the almond milk until just boiling in a small pan or in the microwave then add to the blender, screw on the lid and blitz until smooth.

2 Pour into a bowl and add the mango slices and ginger strips, then scatter the raspberries, almonds, goji berries and chia seeds over the top and serve.

Energy 214kcal/900kJ; Protein 5.7g; Carbohydrate 24.7g, of which sugars 23.5g; Fat 10.9g, of which saturates 1g; Cholesterol 0mg; Calcium 87mg; Fibre 8g; Sodium 137mg.

Green tea, lime and mango soup

SERVES 1

1 matcha teabag

125ml/4floz/½ cup boiling water

75g/3oz/⅓ cup diced mango, defrost if using frozen

Juice ½ lime

75g/3oz/1 small carrot, scrubbed and diced

75g/3oz/½ small trimmed golden beetroot, scrubbed and diced

Slice root ginger, diced

1 tbsp powdered soya protein

For the topping

15g/½oz/about 10 blueberries

½ kiwi fruit, sliced

Little shredded kale

Few ground flaxseeds

A cup of tea takes on a whole new look with this light fresh-tasting, vibrant fruit soup. Green tea is thought to contain more antioxidant polyphenols than black tea, and matcha is a very concentrated powdered form.

1 Add the teabag to a mug, pour over the boiling water and leave to brew for a minute or two.

2 Remove the teabag from the water then add the tea to a blender goblet with the mango and lime juice, carrot, beetroot, ginger and soya protein. Screw on the lid and blitz until smooth.

3 Warm the soup in a pan or in the microwave. Pour into a big cup or bowl and decorate with the blueberries, kiwi fruit, kale and flaxseeds.

Energy 119kcal/507kJ; Protein 2.6g; Carbohydrate 27.6g, of which sugars 25.8g; Fat 0.6g, of which saturates 0.1g; Cholesterol 0mg; Calcium 50mg; Fibre 8.1g; Sodium 71mg.

Spiced apple and apricot soup

Our grannies used to say, 'an apple a day keeps the doctor away'. While this everyday fruit does not contain as much vitamin C as some other fruits it does provide powerful antioxidants – these are found mainly in the skin, along with pectin, a soluble fibre that binds with soluble fat to help lower cholesterol levels and aid heart health.

1 Add the apple, apricots and water to a medium pan. Break the cardamom pod open then add the pod and tiny black seeds to the pan with the cinnamon. Bring the water to the boil, cover the pan and simmer gently for 5–10 minutes until the apple is soft.

2 Discard the cardamom pod, leaving the black seeds in the pan. Tip the fruit mix and water into a blender goblet, add the orange juice then screw on the lid and blend until smooth. Adjust with a little extra boiling water if very thick then spoon the soup into a bowl. Decorate with the cranberries.

NUTRIENT NOTE Dried apricots make a handy standby; naturally sweet, they are a good source of fibre to help promote and maintain blood glucose and cholesterol levels, plus they contain beta-carotene to aid good eyesight and the essential minerals iron, potassium and calcium. They are available in two types, the brighter apricot-coloured ready-to-eat dried apricots or the naturally sun-dried fruits that are much darker in colour and require soaking in cold water before use.
COOK'S TIP As an alternative topping sprinkle on 3 tbsp of honeyed granola, see p29, breaking the pieces into smaller bits if needed, a little finely grated orange zest and a pinch of ground cinnamon.

SERVES 1

1 dessert apple, cored, no need to peel, and diced

50g/2oz/generous ¼ cup ready-to-eat dried apricots

125ml/4fl oz/½ cup water

1 cardamom pod, crushed

Pinch ground cinnamon

Juice ½ medium orange

For the topping
2 tsp dried cranberries

Energy 160kcal/682kJ; Protein 3.2g; Carbohydrate 38.2g, of which sugars 38.2g; Fat 0.5g, of which saturates 0g; Cholesterol 0mg; Calcium 74mg; Fibre 7.4g; Sodium 14mg.

Yellow peril soup

SERVES 1

100ml/3½fl oz/scant ½ cup water

50g/2oz/¼ cup reduced-fat canned coconut milk

40g/1½oz/¼ cup frozen corn

½ small yellow (bell) pepper, cored, deseeded and diced

110g/4oz or 1 thin slice pineapple, peel cut away, cored and diced

1 tsp chia seeds

¼ fresh lime

For the topping

2 cauliflower florets, cut into small pieces

2 tsp roughly chopped pistachio nuts

Torn nasturtium or English marigold petals, optional

Few small rocket (arugula) leaves, optional

This bright yellow smoothie-style soup is a mix of corn, yellow pepper and pineapple for a high fibre, vitamin- and antioxidant-boosting pick-me-up.

1 Add the water, coconut milk and corn to a small pan and simmer for 3 minutes until the corn is hot.

2 Reserve a little of the yellow pepper for the topping then add the rest to a blender goblet with the pineapple. Pour in the coconut and corn mix, screw on the lid and blend until smooth. Stir in the chia seeds and add lime juice to taste.

3 Pour into a bowl, and top with the reserved yellow pepper, cauliflower florets, pistachio nuts, flower petals and rocket leaves, if using.

NUTRIENT NOTE Packed with good carbs, corn is digested slowly by the body so leaving you feeling fuller and energized for longer.
COOK'S TIP If this soup is left to stand the chia seeds will swell and it will take on a jelly-like texture, so serve it as soon as it is made.

Energy 183kcal/773kJ; Protein 6.1g; Carbohydrate 27.6g, of which sugars 20.9g; Fat 6g, of which saturates 0.9g; Cholesterol 0mg; Calcium 81mg; Fibre 8.2g; Sodium 138mg.

Moroccan mint soup

Mint is one of the oldest herbs, first used by the Ancient Greeks and Romans to help relieve pain. Mixed with spinach, grapes and kiwi fruit it makes an eyecatching, refreshing and super-healthy fruit soup.

1 Add the mint leaves to a cup, pour over the boiling water and leave to infuse for a minute or two.

2 Pour the mint tea and leaves into a blender goblet, add the spinach, grapes and kiwi fruit. Screw on the lid and blitz until smooth.

3 Pour into a bowl, drizzle with the yogurt, and top with the raspberries and pomegranate seeds before sprinkling with the nuts, a few pumpkin seeds and a few extra mint leaves.

NUTRIENT NOTE Fresh mint acts as a mouth and breath freshener. It also aids digestion and helps ease the symptoms of indigestion and inflammation, and is often included on detox diets. It also contains trace elements of iron, potassium and vitamin A.

COOK'S TIP Mix and match the smoothie toppings depending on what you have in the refrigerator.

SERVES 1

10 mint leaves

125ml/4fl oz/½ cup boiling water

15g/½oz/½ cup baby spinach leaves

40g/1½oz/scant ¼ cup seedless green grapes

1 kiwi fruit, peeled and sliced

For the topping

1 tbsp fat-free natural yogurt

6 raspberries

1 tbsp fresh pomegranate seeds

2 tsp cashew or pistachio nuts, roughly chopped

Few pumpkin seeds

Few extra mint leaves

Energy 98kcal/415kJ; Protein 3.2g; Carbohydrate 15.6g, of which sugars 15.2g; Fat 3g, of which saturates 0.4g; Cholesterol 0mg; Calcium 81mg; Fibre 3.5g; Sodium 59mg.

LAYERED BREAKFASTS

Assemble delicious layers of healthy ingredients in clip-top and mason screw-top jars and take them with you for a healthy breakfast to go. Choose from luscious creamy probiotic low-fat yogurt or vanilla cashew nut cream; bircher-style oats; fruit purées speckled with chia seeds; and multi-coloured layers of grated beetroot, apple, kale, velvety smooth avocado and summer berries. Superfood stripes in a jar!

Bircher muesli pots

Make the pots the day before, even two days in advance, add a well-fitting lid and keep in the refrigerator ready and waiting for a colourful fruit topping to be added.

1 Add the nuts, seeds, oats and cinnamon to a bowl and stir together. Add the grated apple, yogurt and orange juice then stir together.

2 Divide the mixture evenly between 6 small glass pots with lids and smooth the tops level. Cover and chill in the refrigerator until ready to serve.

TOPPINGS, EACH ENOUGH FOR 2 POTS

Very berrytastic Purée 100g/3¾oz hulled strawberries in a blender until smooth. Spoon over the pots and divide the toppings of 15g/½oz/or 10 blueberries and 25g/1oz/or 4 blackberries.

Mango and chia Purée 100g/3¾oz prepared mango flesh with 2 tbsp lime or orange juice or water in a blender until smooth. Stir in ½ tsp chia seeds then spoon over the top of the pots and decorate with a few pomegranate seeds.

Banana, cacao and coconut Mix 4 tbsp fat-free natural Greek (US strained plain) yogurt with 1 tbsp cacao powder and 2 tsp date syrup or honey, and spoon over the pots. Top with each with ¼ small sliced banana, a few roughly chopped goji berries and a sprinkling of coconut flakes.

Green dream Peel and dice 1 kiwi fruit and mix with 25g/1oz/8 green seedless grapes, halved. Spoon over the top of the pots.

Red peril Purée 100g/3¾oz hulled strawberries in a blender until smooth. Spoon over the pots and top each with 4 raspberries and a couple of hulled and halved strawberries.

MAKES 6

50g/2oz/⅓ cup mixed unblanched hazelnuts, almonds and Brazil nuts, roughly chopped

4 tsp ground flaxseeds

110g/4oz/1 cup jumbo rolled oats

¼ tsp ground cinnamon

1 dessert apple, cored and coarsely grated, no need to peel

250g/9oz/generous 1 cup fat-free natural yogurt or dairy-free alternative

4 tbsp fresh orange juice

Base: Energy 28kcal/119kJ; Protein 1.1g; Carbohydrate 3.4g, of which sugars 0.9g; Fat 1.2g, of which saturates 0.1g; Cholesterol 0mg; Calcium 16mg; Fibre 0.5g; Sodium 7.6mg. **Berrytastic:** Energy 10.5kcal/44kJ; Protein 0.25g; Carbohydrate 2.4g, of which sugars 2.2g; Fat 0.05g, of which saturates 0g; Cholesterol 0mg; Calcium 6.5mg; Fibre 0.75g; Sodium 2mg. **Mango:** Energy 18kcal/76kJ; Protein 0.35g; Carbohydrate 3.7g, of which sugars 3.6g; Fat 0.3g, of which saturates 0.05g; Cholesterol 0mg; Calcium 7mg; Fibre 1.2g; Sodium 7mg. **Banana:** Energy 34kcal/143.5kJ; Protein 1.25g; Carbohydrate 6.8g, of which sugars 6.35g; Fat 0.4g, of which saturates 0.05g; Cholesterol 0mg; Calcium 27mg; Fibre 0.4g; Sodium 25.5mg. **Green:** Energy 11kcal/47kJ; Protein 0.2g; Carbohydrate 2.55g, of which sugars 2.5g; Fat 0.1g, of which saturates 0g; Cholesterol 0mg; Calcium 4.5mg; Fibre 0.45g; Sodium 1mg. **Red:** Energy 9kcal/37kJ; Protein 0.3g; Carbohydrate 1.9g, of which sugars 1/9g; Fat 0.05g, of which saturates 0g; Cholesterol 0mg; Calcium 6mg; Fibre 0.65g; Sodium 2mg.

Traffic light layers

With brightly coloured layers of concentrated fruity goodness, rich in vitamin C, cancer-fighting antioxidants and natural energy-boosting fruit sugars, starches and fibre, this is a healthy fresh-tasting start to the day. Make and enjoy one right now and keep the other glass in the refrigerator for breakfast tomorrow.

1 Add the avocado, spinach and lime juice to the blender goblet, screw on the lid and blitz until smooth. Spoon into the bases of 2 glass tumblers and sprinkle with half the oats.

2 Rinse out the blender goblet then add the grapefruit and still-frozen mango and blitz until smooth. Carefully spoon over the green layer in the glasses and sprinkle with the rest of the oats.

3 Rinse out the blender goblet once more then add the beetroot and raspberries, screw on the lid and blitz until smooth, adding a little water if needed. Spoon over the mango then decorate the top with extra whole berries if liked.

COOK'S TIP Frozen ready-prepared fruit make a handy standby: either buy ready-prepared and ready-frozen or make up your own packs when fruits are in season or on special offer. With a storage life of a month or two there's no need to worry about the fruit going soft before you get around to using them. There is no need to defrost before you use them, just blitz with other non-frozen ingredients for a creamy smooth, almost ice cream–like, texture.

SERVES 2

Green layer
½ ripe avocado, stoned (pitted) and flesh scooped from shell
25g/1oz/1 cup baby spinach leaves
Juice ½ small lime
3 tbsp rolled oats

Yellow layer
½ white grapefruit, peeled weight 110g/4oz, roughly chopped
50g/2oz/⅓ cup frozen mango, diced

Red layer
75g/3oz or 1 small trimmed beetroot, scrubbed and diced
50g/2oz/½ cup fresh or frozen raspberries, plus few extra to decorate, optional

Energy 96kcal/403.5kJ; Protein 2.6g; Carbohydrate 14.1g, of which sugars 5.65g; Fat 3.6g, of which saturates 0.55g; Cholesterol 0mg; Calcium 33mg; Fibre 3.6g; Sodium 27mg.

2 large strawberries, hulled
and sliced

½ vanilla pod (bean), slit and
seeds scraped from pod,
or ¼ tsp vanilla extract

110g/4oz/scant ½ cup
fat-free Greek (US strained
plain) yogurt or dairy-free
alternative

1 tsp shelled hemp seeds,
plus a few extra for topping

25g/1oz/scant ¼ cup
blueberries

6 raspberries

½ tsp sunflower seeds

Taste of summer in a pot

Plain Greek yogurt gets the designer makeover in this
super-easy layered breakfast. It's rich in healthy
probiotic bacteria and bone-building calcium, plus
vitamin C-boosting strawberries, blueberries and
raspberries to help enhance immunity and fight infection.

1 Stand a ring of sliced strawberries inside the base of the
glass then fill the centre with the remaining slices.

2 Stir the vanilla into the yogurt then spoon over the
strawberries and sprinkle the top with hemp seeds. Arrange
a layer of blueberries on top.

3 Mash the raspberries with a fork on a plate. Spoon on top
of the blueberries, sprinkle with the sunflower seeds and a
few extra hemp seeds, and serve.

NUTRIENT TIP Choose shelled hemp seeds rather than the whole
seeds as these are easier for the body to break down and absorb
the nutrients that they contain.

Energy 198kcal/829kJ; Protein 10.4g; Carbohydrate 20.1g, of which sugars 14.9g; Fat 8.9g, of which saturates 1.3g; Cholesterol 0mg; Calcium 205mg; Fibre 4.6g; Sodium 91mg.

Vanilla prunes with banana layers

Prunes are delicious, yet many of us have a love or hate relationship with this fibre-rich dried fruit. We need fibre to keep our digestive tract running smoothly and it also helps to reduce cholesterol. Prunes contain high levels of phenoic and flavonoid compounds which, with the vitamin K they contain, may also help to slow down bone loss and aid circulation as we age.

1 Add the prunes, water and vanilla to a blender goblet, screw on the lid and blend until smooth. Spoon the prunes into a small bowl or if you have a second blender goblet, leave them in the goblet.

2 Reserve a few banana slices for decoration and add the rest to a clean blender goblet with the cashew nut pieces, screw on the lid and blend until smooth. Add the yogurt and mix very briefly.

3 Spoon 2 tbsp granola into the base of a glass tumbler, spoon over a little of the banana mix then add half the prunes. Spoon over more banana mix, the remaining prunes then the last of the banana mix. Marble the layers together with a skewer, if liked. Sprinkle the rest of the granola over the top with the reserved banana slices, and serve.

COOK'S TIP If you don't have time to make your own granola then buy a good quality shop-bought one and sprinkle with a little ground cacao powder.

SERVES 1

40g/1½oz/or 5 small pitted ready-to-eat prunes, chopped

4 tbsp water

Few drops vanilla extract

½ small banana, 50g/2oz peeled weight, sliced

2 tbsp cashew nut pieces

4 tbsp fat-free Greek (US strained plain) yogurt or dairy-free alternative

30g/1¼oz/3 tbsp fruity cacao granola, see p30

Energy 420kcal/1761kJ; Protein 13.3g; Carbohydrate 48.8g, of which sugars 37.2g; Fat 20.4g, of which saturates 1.8g; Cholesterol 0mg; Calcium 202mg; Fibre 5.7g; Sodium 68mg.

Roasted peach layers with date honey

SERVES 1

1 ripe peach, halved, stoned (pitted) and diced

Juice ½ small orange

175g/6oz/¾ cup fat-free Greek (US strained plain) yogurt or dairy-free alternative

2 tsp ground flaxseeds

Few drops orange flower water, optional

1 tbsp rolled oats, plus a few extra for topping

1–2 tsp date honey

2 tsp pistachio nuts, roughly chopped

Few dried goji berries

A wonderful combo of hot peaches with a tang of orange, layered with cool creamy calcium-rich Greek yogurt and a drizzle of dark sticky date honey.

1 Line the grill or broiling pan with a piece of foil, turn up the edges to make a small tray then add the diced peach and orange juice. Grill for 4–5 minutes until the peach is hot and just beginning to brown a little around the edges.

2 Meanwhile mix the yogurt with the flaxseeds and orange flower water to taste, if using.

3 Spoon the oats into the base of a glass. Spoon half the hot peaches on top then spoon over half the yogurt. Drizzle with a little of the date honey then repeat with a second layer of the remaining peaches and yogurt.

4 Drizzle with a little more date honey. Sprinkle with the pistachio nuts, goji berries and a few more oats, and serve immediately.

COOK'S TIP Date honey, sometimes called date syrup, is a thick brown sweet syrup that looks a little like molasses or dark maple syrup and is made by slowly simmering fresh dates in water then squeezing out the juice and simmering again until it becomes a thick syrup. It is popular in North African and Middle Eastern cooking but it is especially popular in Israel where it has been made for hundreds of years. You can use in place of honey for those on a vegan diet, in sweet or savoury recipes.

Energy 281kcal/1191kJ; Protein 14.1g; Carbohydrate 39.2g, of which sugars 24.8g; Fat 8.7g, of which saturates 1.8g; Cholesterol 2mg; Calcium 305mg; Fibre 7.1g; Sodium 170mg.

Rainbow in a jar

We are always encouraged to eat more vegetables and fruit, and this colourful breakfast in a jar is the perfect energizing, protein-, vitamin- and mineral-boosting way to do it.

1 Spoon the muesli into the base of a clip-top jar then drizzle the 3 tbsp water over the top. Spoon the grated apple into an even layer then top with the kale and then the beetroot.

2 Add the mango and water to a blender, screw on the lid and blend until smooth. Spoon over the beetroot then top with a spoonful of the cashew cream and a sprinkling of spirulina. Serve now or clip the lid in place and take to work.

NUTRIENT NOTE Health professionals recommend that we eat five 75g/3oz portions of vegetables and fruit a day, but many of us don't actually manage it. The average consumption is nearer three portions. This healthy breakfast provides three in just one meal!

COOK'S TIP If you don't have any cashew cream then top with a spoonful of soya vanilla-flavoured yogurt, or stir a few drops of vanilla extract into a little fat-free Greek (US strained plain) yogurt.

SERVES 1

25g/1oz/¼ cup nut muesli, see p28

3 tbsp water

1 dessert apple, cored, no need to peel, coarsely grated

15g/½oz/½ cup kale, very finely shredded

50g/2oz/1 small trimmed, scrubbed beetroot, coarsely grated

75g/3oz/⅓ cup frozen mango, just defrosted and diced

1 tbsp water

1 tbsp homemade cashew cream, see p33

Pinch ground spirulina

Energy 260kcal/1097kJ; Protein 6.7g; Carbohydrate 37.2g, of which sugars 23g; Fat 10.4g, of which saturates 5.1g; Cholesterol 0mg; Calcium 56mg; Fibre 8.1g; Sodium 51mg.

SERVES 1

50g/2oz/¼ cup fromage frais or fat-free Greek (US strained plain) yogurt or dairy-free alternative

2 tsp raw cacao powder, plus a little extra to decorate

1 tsp hazelnut or almond butter

1 small banana, 100g/3¾oz peeled weight, sliced

1 small ripe peach, stoned (pitted) and chopped

1 tbsp water

20g/¾oz/2 tbsp fruity cacao granola, see p30

4 frozen raspberries, just defrosted

1 small ice cube of raspberry purée, see p13, defrosted

Nutty chocolate fruit shots

There is something decadent about a chocolate fix for breakfast but rather than reaching for the ultra-sweet, highly refined breakfast cereal, opt for this healthy antioxidant-boosting raw cacao-, calcium- and vitamin C-brimming option instead.

1 Add the fromage frais or yogurt to a small bowl then stir in the cacao powder and nut butter. Mash the banana with a fork then stir into the cacao mixture and spoon into the base of a glass tumbler or clip-top jar.

2 Reserve a small portion of peach and add the rest with the water to a blender goblet, screw on the lid and blitz together until smooth. Spoon over the cacao layer then sprinkle with the granola. Top with the reserved peach, raspberries and raspberry purée, and serve.

NUTRIENT NOTE On average a small 100g/3¾oz peach contains around 30 calories. It is rich in vitamin C and fibre, providing you don't remove the skin. When canned, peaches lose 80% of their vitamin C, so try to eat fresh or frozen every time.

Energy 194kcal/821kJ; Protein 7.5g; Carbohydrate 32.7g, of which sugars 29.7g; Fat 4.6g, of which saturates 0.9g; Cholesterol 1mg; Calcium 92mg; Fibre 4.7g; Sodium 59mg.

Cinnamon plums with cranberry trail mix

So that you can quickly and easily put together this tasty layered breakfast you might like to double, or even quadruple the plum compote and store in the refrigerator in individual sized clip-topped jars, or plastic containers if you want to freeze them. Just add yogurt and trail mix layers in the morning, to eat at once or seal with a lid and take to work.

1 Add the plums, honey or maple syrup, water and cinnamon to a small pan. Cover and simmer gently for 4–5 minutes until soft. Put to one side to cool.

2 Spoon the plums into a glass tumbler, clip-top jar or plastic container, top with the yogurt and sprinkle over the trail mix.

COOK'S TIP You might also like to make this up with a mix of plums and blackberries or blueberries, apple and blackberries.

SERVES 1

2 ripe red plums, halved, stoned (pitted) and sliced

1 tsp clear honey or maple syrup

3 tbsp water

Large pinch ground cinnamon

75g/3oz/⅓ cup fat-free Greek (US strained plain) yogurt or dairy-free alternative

25g/1oz/¼ cup cranberry trail mix, see below

CRANBERRY TRAIL MIX
(Makes 130g/4½oz/1 generous cup)
Mix 2 tbsp each of dried cranberries, dried goji berries, dried coconut flakes, pumpkin seeds, sunflower seeds, and unblanched almonds that have been roughly chopped with 2 tsp hulled hemp seeds and 2 tsp ground flaxseeds. Spoon into a clip-top jar and keep in the refrigerator for up to 2 weeks.

Energy 204kcal/858kJ; Protein 7.8g; Carbohydrate 25.4g, of which sugars 24.7g; Fat 8.6g, of which saturates 0.7g; Cholesterol 0mg; Calcium 174mg; Fibre 1.5g; Sodium 59mg.

SMOOTHIE BOWLS

Smoothies are taken one step further here with bright and bold fruity toppings, crisp golden granolas, crunchy chopped nuts and seeds, and sprinkles of vibrant green spirulina or wheatgrass, purple chia powder or eye-catching goji berries. Arrange in swirls, stripes, patterns or simply scatter the toppings over. Bring out the artist in you and wake up the senses in every way. Breakfast will never be the same again.

Cacao and banana with maple seeds

SERVES 1

1 small banana, sliced

4 tsp vanilla protein powder

2 tsp raw cacao powder

2 tsp ground flaxseeds

2 tsp cashew or hazelnut butter

25g/1oz/1 cup baby spinach leaves or shredded red chard

90ml/3fl oz/⅓ cup unsweetened almond milk

For the topping

1 tsp dried goji berries

½ quantity maple-glazed seed brittle, see below

A rich dark chocolatey fix, this smoothie bowl is made with almond milk and is packed with protein boosters, and topped with an easy maple-glazed seed brittle for a crunchy mineral-rich finish.

1 Reserve half the banana slices for decoration then add the rest to the blender goblet with the protein powder, cacao, flaxseeds and nut butter. Add the spinach or chard and almond milk, screw on the lid and blend until smooth.

2 Pour into a bowl then top with the reserved banana slices, goji berries and maple-glazed seeds, and serve.

NUTRIENT NOTE – if you are on a dairy-free diet make sure to check the label on the vanilla protein powder, as some can be whey- or dairy-based.

MAPLE GLAZED SEED BRITTLE
(Serves 2)
1 Add 1 tbsp sunflower seeds, 1 tbsp pumpkin seeds and 1 tbsp sesame seeds to a small dry frying pan and cook for 2–3 minutes over a medium heat until just beginning to colour. Add 4 tsp maple syrup and cook for a minute or two more, stirring until the syrup is bubbling and the sesame seeds are golden.
2 Tip out on to a baking sheet lined with a piece of baking parchment and spread into a thin layer. Leave to cool and harden for 15 minutes or longer if time, then break into pieces. Wrap what you are not using straight away in foil and store in the refrigerator for up to 3 days.

Energy 297kcal/1250kJ; Protein 22.4g; Carbohydrate 29.5g, of which sugars 23.3g; Fat 10.3g, of which saturates 1.2g; Cholesterol 0mg; Calcium 54mg; Fibre 6.7g; Sodium 158mg.

Gorgeous green bowl

This vibrant green bowl just screams out that it is good for you. It is packed with energy-boosting avocado and pear for a velvety smoothness plus antioxidant-, mineral- and vitamin-boosting green leaves and kiwi, to enhance immunity and health.

1 Add the kale and spinach to a blender goblet then add half the avocado, pear and kiwi. Pour in the almond milk, screw on the lid and blitz until smooth.

2 Pour the smoothie into a bowl. Arrange the remaining sliced avocado, pear and kiwi over the top of the smoothie. Add the alfalfa sprouts to the centre then sprinkle with the seeds and goji berries and serve.

NUTRIENT NOTE Sprouting seeds make great toppings for smoothie bowls. As the seeds begin to sprout their natural nutrients increase massively to meet the growing needs of the young shoots, making them nutrient-dense yet easy to digest. Buy ready-sprouted in small packs in the supermarket or grow your own at home.

SERVES 1

15g/½oz/½ cup shredded kale

25g/1oz/1 cup baby spinach leaves

½ medium avocado, stoned (pitted), peeled and sliced

½ small pear, no need to peel, cored and sliced

1 kiwi fruit, peeled and sliced

125ml/4fl oz/½ cup unsweetened almond milk

For the topping
1 tbsp alfalfa sprouts
2 tsp pumpkin seeds
1 tsp goji berries

Energy 337kcal/1133kJ; Protein 6.6g; Carbohydrate 21.9g, of which sugars 18.1g; Fat 19.6g, of which saturates 3.6g; Cholesterol 0mg; Calcium 95mg; Fibre 8.6g; Sodium 135mg.

Bowl of cherryaid

SERVES 1

110g/3¾oz fresh or frozen pitted cherries

1 medium trimmed beetroot, about 100g/3½oz, peeled and diced

15g/½oz/½ cup shredded kale

Large pinch ground cinnamon

125ml/4fl oz/½ cup water

For the topping

1 tsp sunflower seeds

1 tsp ground flaxseeds

1 tsp goji berries

2 tsp rolled oats

Few blueberries

Few sun-dried mulberries, optional

Few tiny edible flowers such as violas or herb flowers, optional

Frozen ready-prepared cherries make a great healthy addition to this amazingly coloured deep red smoothie. There's no need to defrost them first, just blitz with beetroot, kale and a hint of cinnamon for a vitalizing and energy-boosting bowl.

1 Add the cherries, beetroot, kale, cinnamon and water to a blender goblet. Screw on the lid and blitz until smooth.

2 Pour the smoothie into a bowl and top with the seeds, goji berries, oats and then the blueberries. Decorate with mulberries and flowers, if using, and serve.

NUTRIENT NOTE Beetroot is a powerhouse of antioxidants and nutrients. It includes the folates vital for new cell growth and DNA, so important for pregnant women, along with other B vitamins and small amounts of vitamin C, plus the minerals iron, manganese, copper and magnesium with smaller amounts of potassium. The good carbs will help to fight fatigue and boost energy. The pigment betacyanin gives beetroot its deep red colour and works with manganese and vitamin C to aid good eye health and overall tissue health and may even help to reduce the oxidation of LDL cholesterol, so helping to reduce the risk of heart disease.

COOK'S TIP Look out for mulberries in sealed pouches in the health food store, they look a little like a dried brown raspberry but add a great natural sweet hit to any smoothie bowl.

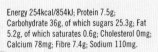

Energy 254kcal/854kJ; Protein 7.5g; Carbohydrate 36g, of which sugars 25.3g; Fat 5.2g, of which saturates 0.6g; Cholesterol 0mg; Calcium 78mg; Fibre 7.4g; Sodium 110mg.

SERVES 1

1 kiwi fruit, peeled, diced

50g/2oz/⅓ cup frozen sliced bananas

50g/2oz/⅓ cup frozen mango, diced

4 little gem lettuce leaves

125ml/4fl oz/½ cup coconut water

½ tsp wheatgrass powder

For the topping

1 small ice cube of raspberry purée, see p13, defrosted

25g/1oz/2 frozen mango, cut into small dice

Few whole raspberries

Few hulled hemp seeds

Few tiny feathery rocket (arugula) leaves or a little shredded lettuce

Tropical sensation in a bowl

Adding a mix of fresh and frozen fruit to a smoothie gives a texture like soft scoop ice cream, which is deliciously refreshing and helps to cut down on the amount of prep needed. There is no need to defrost frozen fruit first, just add a handful to the blender and away you go.

1 Reserve one quarter of the kiwi fruit for the topping and add the rest to the goblet of a blender with the banana slices, mango and lettuce. Pour in the coconut water and add the wheatgrass powder. Screw on the lid and blend until smooth.

2 Pour into a bowl, decorate with a swirl of raspberry purée, the remaining kiwi fruit, diced mango and a few whole raspberries then sprinkle with the hemp seeds and rocket or lettuce and serve.

COOK'S NOTE Bananas are very popular and can almost always be found in a fruit bowl, yet they have only a short storage life. If you haven't eaten as many as you had expected, don't let them go past their best: peel, slice and arrange on a baking sheet and freeze for 3–4 hours until hard. Transfer to a plastic bag, seal and label. Mangoes, cherries and summer berry fruits are readily available frozen in the supermarket, or make up your own fruit packs just like the frozen bananas. Freeze bananas up to 1 month, other fruits up to 6 months.

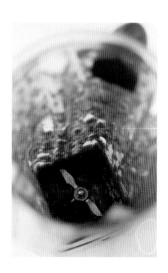

Energy 124kcal/527kJ; Protein 2g; Carbohydrate 29.3g, of which sugars 27.7g; Fat 0.6g, of which saturates 0.1g; Cholesterol 0mg; Calcium 31mg; Fibre 5.4g; Sodium 5mg.

Apple and blackberry crumble bowl

SERVES 1

1 dessert apple, no need
to peel, quartered, cored,
dice ¾ and slice ¼

1 small ripe pear, no need to
peel, cored and diced

125g/4¼oz/½ cup low-fat
natural yogurt

Little vanilla extract

For the topping

40g/1½oz/⅓ cup nut muesli,
see p28

1 frozen ice cube of
blackberry purée, see p13,
defrosted

Few fresh or frozen
blackberries, just defrosted
if frozen

All the flavours of apple crumble but with none of the
refined carbs. Instead, healthy homemade high-fibre, high-
energy nut muesli and soothing low-fat natural yogurt.

1 Add the diced apple, pear, yogurt and vanilla to a blender
goblet, screw on the lid and blend until smooth. Pour into
a bowl.

2 Spoon the muesli into the centre of the bowl. Top with the
apple slices. Spoon dots of blackberry purée on the smoothie
bowl, sprinkle with a few extra blackberries and serve.

NUTRIENT NOTE Apples and pears are rich in pectin, the setting
agent in jam which also helps to remove bad cholesterol from the
body. They also stimulate the growth of friendly bacteria in the large
intestine, boost vitamin C and contain the simple sugar fructose,
which is sweeter than sucrose found in sugar cane but metabolized
by the body more slowly.

COOK'S TIP Apples and pears quickly oxidize and go brown so
make sure to serve this smoothie bowl the moment you have made it.

Energy 308kcal/1302kJ; Protein 13.7g; Carbohydrate 48.3g, of which sugars 26.1g; Fat 8g, of which saturates 0.9g; Cholesterol 0mg; Calcium 236mg; Fibre 7.4g; Sodium 105mg.

Spinach and spirulina smoothie bowl

SERVES 1

25g/1oz/1 cup baby spinach leaves

15g/½oz/½ cup shredded kale

1 small banana, sliced

125ml/4fl oz/½ cup pressed cloudy apple juice

¼ tsp spirulina, plus little extra to decorate

1 tbsp dried sea salad, plus little extra to decorate

For the topping

2 strawberries, hulled and sliced

1 tsp sunflower seeds

1 tsp hemp oil

NUTRIENT NOTE Spinach and kale contain a high concentration of carotenoids – spinach has beta–carotene and lutein and kale has lutein and zeaxanthin. These appear to have important antioxidant properties.
COOK'S TIP Kale can be a little overpowering, mixing with a little naturally sweet banana helps to balance and complement the flavours.

This smoothie bowl has one of the most striking colours, a bold deep green from antioxidant-rich spinach and kale, then supercharged with protein-boosting spirulina and mineral-rich sea salad. Adding a little banana helps to sweeten and balance the kale which can sometimes be a little strong.

1 Add the baby spinach and shredded kale to a blender goblet with half the sliced banana. Pour in the apple juice then add the spirulina and dried sea salad. Screw on the lid and blend until smooth.

2 Pour into a bowl then decorate the top with the remaining sliced banana and strawberries. Sprinkle with a little extra spirulina and sea salad and the sunflower seeds then drizzle with the hemp oil. Serve immediately.

Energy 215kcal/908kJ; Protein 3.6g; Carbohydrate 38.6g, of which sugars 35.4g; Fat 6.1g, of which saturates 0.9g; Cholesterol 0mg; Calcium 92mg; Fibre 3.3g; Sodium 61mg.

Papaya and orange wake-up bowl

SERVES 1

½ small papaya, seeds discarded, peeled and diced (prepared weight about 100g/3¾oz)

1 small carrot 75g/3oz, scrubbed and sliced

2 tsp ground flaxseeds

Juice 1 medium orange

For the topping

2 tbsp muesli base, see p28

4 unblanched almonds, halved

2 strawberries, hulled and sliced

Few blueberries

Awaken the senses with this taste sensation, creamy smooth papaya with the tang of fresh citrus orange then topped with crunchy muesli and summer berries. A picture in a bowl.

1 Add the papaya, carrot, flaxseeds and orange juice to a blender goblet. Screw on the lid and blitz until smooth.

2 Pour into a bowl and decorate with the muesli base, almonds, strawberries and blueberries then serve.

NUTRIENT NOTE Half a papaya contains an adult's daily allowance of vitamin C, needed to produce white blood cells to help fight infection and to produce collagen for healthy muscles, skin and bones.
COOK'S TIP If you have some frozen cubes of fruit purée in the freezer, see p13, you might like to defrost one and drizzle over the smoothie bowl just before serving.

Energy 286kcal/1198kJ; Protein 8.6g; Carbohydrate 37.2g, of which sugars 22.8g; Fat 12.3g, of which saturates 1.2g; Cholesterol 0mg; Calcium 91mg; Fibre 11.3g; Sodium 68mg.

Acai berry blitz bowl

Acai (pronounced ah-sah-ee) has grown in popularity as the must-have fruit. These small dark purple fruits come from the acai palm tree found in the Amazonian regions of Brazil. Buy as a frozen purée, defrost in the microwave and then purée with kale and banana for this antioxidant-boosting breakfast.

1 Add the acai purée, banana and kale to a blender goblet then add the oats and coconut water. Screw on the lid and blitz until smooth.

2 Pour into a bowl. Top with small blobs of the cashew cream in a ring, then add the blueberries and raspberries, sprinkle with the goji berries and moringa, wheatgrass or spirulina powder, finally scatter over the seeds, and serve.

NUTRIENT NOTE There are some wild claims being made about the health benefits of acai berries from anti-ageing to weight loss. There is little evidence to back this up but they do contain anthocyanins which give them their dark colour; these antioxidants are also found in blueberries and cranberries and are thought to help protect the body from free-radical damage which can lead to cancer.

COOK'S TIP You can buy acai purée in the freezer sections of good health food stores but if you can't find it, use 100g/3¾oz/¾ cup frozen pitted cherries instead. No need to defrost fully if your blender is the kind that is tough enough to blitz ice cubes. Acai berries can also be found in little packets of powder which add a bright splash of colour when sprinkled over a green or orange smoothie bowl.

SERVES 1

100g/3¾oz frozen acai berry purée, defrosted in the microwave for a few minutes to soften slightly

½ small banana, peeled and broken into pieces

15g/½oz/½ cup shredded kale

2 tbsp rolled oats

125ml/4fl oz/½ cup coconut water

For the topping

2 tbsp cashew cream, see p33

Few blueberries

Few raspberries

1 tsp dried goji berries

Pinch moringa, wheatgrass or spirulina powder

Few hulled hemp seeds

Few hulled pumpkin seeds

Energy 321kcal/1347kJ; Protein 7.7g; Carbohydrate 42.3g, of which sugars 18.3g; Fat 14.6g, of which saturates 9.1g; Cholesterol 0mg; Calcium 85mg; Fibre 9.6g; Sodium 30mg.

Avocado and matcha tea bowl

SERVES 1

1 matcha tea bag

175ml/6fl oz/¾ cup boiling water

½ medium ripe avocado, stoned (pitted), peeled and diced

25g/1oz/1 cup baby spinach leaves

1 tbsp dried shredded sea salad

75g/3oz frozen banana slices

Juice ½ lime

For the topping

2 tbsp low-fat natural yogurt or dairy-free alternative

25g/1oz/or 2 chunks frozen mango, just defrosted and diced

Few baby spinach leaves

Few pomegranate seeds

2 tsp pistachio nuts, roughly chopped

2 tsp sunflower seeds

Large pinch spirulina powder, optional

Start the day with healthy green tea, but rather than serve in a cup, use as the base for this avocado, spinach and banana smoothie. If you are in a hurry, brew the tea in half the amount of boiling water then top up with ice cubes.

1 Add the tea bag to a cup, pour over the boiling water and leave to stand for 5 minutes. Remove the tea bag and leave the tea to cool.

2 Pour the cooled tea into a blender goblet, add the avocado, spinach, sea salad, banana slices and lime juice. Screw on the lid and blitz until smooth.

3 Pour into a bowl and add a swirl of yogurt. Top with the mango chunks and spinach leaves then scatter with the pomegranate seeds, nuts and sunflower seeds. Finish with a sprinkle of spirulina, if using.

NUTRIENT NOTE Look out for packs of mixed shredded and dried dulce, nori and sea lettuce in the health food shop. They are rich in iodine needed for normal functioning of the thyroid gland with smaller amounts of copper and iron for healthy blood, magnesium for muscles and nerves, calcium for healthy bones, potassium for fluid balance and zinc for the body's immune system.

COOK'S TIP To make frozen banana slices simply slice bananas and open freeze on a tray lined with baking parchment. Freeze for 3 hours until firm then lift off the paper and add to a plastic bag, squeeze out the air and seal the bag with a clip. Label and freeze for up to a month. Take out as many slices as you need, when you need them, and use straight from the freezer.

Energy 364kcal/1518kJ; Protein 8.5g; Carbohydrate 28.8g, of which sugars 22.4g; Fat 24.6g, of which saturates 4.5g; Cholesterol 0mg; Calcium 111mg; Fibre 7.4g; Sodium 49mg.

Raspberry and watermelon bowl

SERVES 1

75g/3oz/½ cup raspberries

200g/7oz/1 small slice watermelon, peeled, most of the black seeds removed, and diced

75g/3oz/1 small trimmed beetroot, scrubbed and diced

2 tsp ground flaxseeds

1 tsp baobab powder

For the topping

2 tsp cashew cream, see p33

Few tiny baby kale leaves

Few sunflower seeds

Rehydrate with this fab fruity and refreshing smoothie bowl that has just a hint of energy-boosting beetroot.

1 Reserve a few of the raspberries and a little of the watermelon for the topping then add the rest to a blender goblet with the beetroot, flaxseeds and baobab powder. Screw on the lid and blitz until smooth, stirring and scraping down the sides of the goblet once or twice.

2 Spoon into a bowl and add small dots of cashew cream. Top with the reserved raspberries and watermelon then the baby kale leaves and scatter over a few sunflower seeds.

NUTRIENT TIP Watermelon has the lowest calories of all melons at just 30 calories per 100g/3¾oz.

COOK'S TIP Unlike some of the other smoothie bowls you will need to scrape down the sides of the blender as the beetroot takes a while to blitz smooth. You really don't need to add water although you might feel tempted at the beginning; the watermelon will be juicy enough.

Energy 186kcal/791kJ; Protein 5.8g; Carbohydrate 27.5g, of which sugars 23.6g; Fat 6.8g, of which saturates 3g; Cholesterol 0mg; Calcium 49mg; Fibre 8.7g; Sodium 86mg.

Strawberry and chia crush bowl

SERVES 1

150g/5oz/1½ cups
strawberries, hulled

1 small banana, sliced

¼ lemon, diced

½ tsp chia seeds

For the topping

2 tbsp low-fat natural yogurt
or dairy-free alternative

1 tsp hulled hemp seeds

Few extra chia seeds

¼ tsp acai powder, optional

Pretty and pink, this smoothie bowl has a hidden punch with the addition of whole lemon – zingy zest, pith and juicy flesh for the fresh taste that will remind you of summer lemonade.

1 Reserve 1 strawberry and half the banana slices for the topping. Add the rest to a blender goblet with the lemon. Screw on the lid and blend until smooth. Sprinkle in the chia seeds then screw on the lid and blitz again until smooth.

2 Pour into a bowl and swirl in the yogurt. Top with the reserved strawberry, cut into slices, and the remaining banana slices, then sprinkle with the hemp seeds, extra chia seeds and a little acai powder, if using, and serve.

NUTRIENT NOTE Strawberries have more vitamin C than any of the other red summer berries. Although naturally sweet they contain just 27 calories per 100g/3¾oz.

COOK'S TIP Acai powder can be bought in small sachets from the health food store. It is rich in vitamin C and is pale mauve in colour which quickly darkens when in contact with moisture.

Energy 153kcal/647kJ; Protein 4.8g; Carbohydrate
30.7g, of which sugars 27.1g; Fat 2g, of which
saturates 0.2g; Cholesterol 0mg; Calcium 76mg;
Fibre 5.3g; Sodium 46mg.

Blueberry and vanilla smoothie bowl

Dairy-free, yet you certainly don't feel as though you are missing out with this creamy blueberry and banana vanilla-flavoured smoothie. Boosted with healthy oats, seeds and maca, it is then topped with homemade cashew cream for a luxurious start to the day.

1 Add the frozen blueberries, banana and spinach to a blender goblet then add the oats, sunflower seeds and maca. Pour in the almond milk and vanilla extract, then screw on the lid and blend until smooth.

2 Pour into a bowl and top with the cashew cream, the fig wedges, extra blueberries and goji berries, and serve.

NUTRIENT NOTE Blueberries are often called a superfood, rich in antioxidants including anthocyanins that give them their blue colour. They are naturally sweet and bursting with vitamin K and C, plus they contain manganese which helps the body process cholesterol, carbohydrates, protein and phenolic compounds. COOK'S TIP Vary the toppings to suit what you have in the refrigerator, a mix of summer berries or sliced peaches would also taste great.

SERVES 1

75g/3oz/½ cup fresh or frozen blueberries

½ small banana, peeled and broken into pieces

15g/½oz/½ cup baby spinach leaves

1 tbsp rolled oats

1 tbsp sunflower seeds

1 tsp maca powder

125ml/4fl oz/½ cup unsweetened almond milk

Few drops vanilla extract

For the topping

2 tbsp cashew cream, see p33

1 fresh fig, halved, cut into thin wedges

2 tbsp fresh or frozen blueberries, just defrosted if frozen

1 tsp dried goji berries

Energy 459kcal/1650kJ; Protein 8.6g; Carbohydrate 50.6g, of which sugars 30g; Fat 20.6g, of which saturates 10g; Cholesterol 0mg; Calcium 64mg; Fibre 7.4g; Sodium 113mg.

25g/1oz/¼ cup cashew nut pieces

50ml/2fl oz/¼ cup boiling water

100g/3¾oz/¾ cup frozen pitted cherries, no need to defrost

40g/1½oz/generous ¼ cup sliced frozen bananas, no need to defrost

40g/1½oz/1 stem purple sprouting broccoli with leaves, sliced

1 tsp raw cacao powder

125ml/4fl oz/½ cup water

For the topping

2 tbsp muesli base, see p28

1 tsp dried goji berries

1 fresh or frozen cherry, pitted and quartered

1 frozen cube of strawberry purée, defrosted, see p13, or 2 tsp purée

Cacao and cherry bowl

Frozen fruits save time when smoothie making and mean that you always have healthy ingredients at the ready. Keep a jar of homemade muesli in the cupboard and this energizing breakfast can be blitzed together in minutes.

1 Soak the cashew nuts in the boiling water for 5 minutes to soften them slightly. Then add the nuts and soaking water to a blender goblet with the frozen cherries and bananas, the broccoli and cacao powder. Add half the cold water, screw on the lid and blend until smooth. Adjust the consistency with extra water as needed.

2 Pour into a bowl. Top with the muesli base, goji berries and cherry then drizzle with a little strawberry purée and serve.

NUTRIENT NOTE Raw cacao powder comes from cacao beans that have been dried at low temperatures rather than roasted and so contain flavonoid antioxidants which may help protect the body from free-radical damage. As well as containing protein, fibre, vitamins and essential vitamins raw cacao also contains a natural mood enhancer.

Energy 409kcal/1442kJ; Protein 11.9g; Carbohydrate 41.7g, of which sugars 24.7g; Fat 16.9g, of which saturates 3.2g; Cholesterol 0mg; Calcium 60mg; Fibre 6.4g; Sodium 34mg.

Broccoli and avocado wake-up bowl

This guacamole-style smoothie combines everything you should need for a healthy breakfast: good carbs, healthy fats and a mix of vitamins and minerals, with the zing of lime and little fiery chilli to wake-up and kick-start your day.

1 Add the avocado, broccoli and parsley to a blender goblet then add the flaxseeds, almonds and apple juice. Screw on the lid and blend until smooth. Adjust with a little water if very thick and add lime juice to taste.

2 Pour into a bowl. Mix the mango, chopped parsley, chilli and tomato together and spoon into the bowl. Serve immediately sprinkled with a little grated lime zest, a few tiny pieces of broccoli and quartered almonds.

NUTRIENT NOTE Parsley is rich in vitamin K which works with protein to strengthen bones. It is also a good source of calcium and potassium, with smaller amounts of iron and phosphorous.
COOK'S TIP Chillies vary considerably in heat, as a general rule the smaller they are the more hot and fiery they are.

Energy 328kcal/1369kJ; Protein 7.8g; Carbohydrate 22g, of which sugars 17g; Fat 23.9g, of which saturates 3.9g; Cholesterol 0mg; Calcium 66mg; Fibre 9.7g; Sodium 42mg.

SERVES 1

½ medium avocado, stoned (pitted) and flesh scooped from shell

40g/1½oz/3 small broccoli florets, plus a few extra tiny pieces for topping

2 stems fresh parsley

2 tsp ground flaxseeds

10g/¼oz/or 10 unblanched almonds, plus a few extra quartered for topping

120ml/4fl oz/½ cup cloudy pressed apple juice

Juice ¼ lime, to taste

For the topping

25g/1oz/or 2 frozen chunks mango, cut into small dice, no need to defrost

1 tsp fresh chopped parsley

1 slice red chilli, deseeded, finely chopped, or to taste

1 cherry tomato, diced

Little grated lime zest

Buckwheat berry blast bowl

SERVES 1

40g/1½oz/¼ cup buckwheat groats, soaked overnight in cold water

50g/2oz/⅓ cup blueberries

50g/2oz/⅓ cup raspberries

15g/½oz/½ cup baby spinach leaves

½ small banana, peeled and sliced

2 tsp almond butter

125ml/4fl oz/½ cup unsweetened almond milk

For the topping

1 tsp pumpkin seeds

½ tsp acai berry powder

Buckwheat adds a high-fibre and mineral boost to this healthy smoothie bowl. Look out for this tiny triangular nutty-tasting ingredient in the health food shop. Soak in cold water overnight to soften, then blend with fresh fruity berries and spinach for an alternative to bircher muesli or porridge.

1 Drain the buckwheat and add to a blender goblet. Reserve a few of the berries and add the rest to the blender with the spinach, banana, almond butter and milk. Screw on the lid and blend until smooth, adding a little water if needed.

2 Pour into a mug or bowl and decorate with the reserved berries. Sprinkle with the pumpkin seeds and acai berry powder and serve.

NUTRIENT NOTE Fibre is an important part of our diet, yet it is only found in plant-based foods. It not only leaves you feeling fuller for longer but can help to prevent heart disease, diabetes, weight gain and some cancers as well as improving digestive health.

Energy 373kcal/1574kJ; Protein 10.9g; Carbohydrate 56.5g, of which sugars 20.9g; Fat 13.8g, of which saturates 1.2g; Cholesterol 0mg; Calcium 65mg; Fibre 10.3g; Sodium 121mg.

Carrot cake in a bowl

A twist on the traditional carrot cake, this easy-to-make smoothie bowl is a great way to include 2 portions of the recommended fruit and veg for the day without even trying.

1 Add the carrot, apple, ginger and cinnamon to a blender goblet. Pour in the water and add the cashew cream then screw on the lid and blend until smooth.

2 Pour into a bowl. Mix the cashew cream with a little water then swirl over the top of the smoothie. Sprinkle with the cacao granola, the sliced date and a sprinkling of cinnamon. Top with the carrot ribbons and serve.

NUTRIENT NOTE Carrots have tough cellular walls but blending helps to make them easier for the body to digest and convert the beta-carotene they contain into vitamin A, which helps to maintain good health, nourish the skin and help fight the signs of ageing. Herbalists believe carrots have detoxifying properties.
COOKS TIP If you don't have any cashew cream then add 4 unblanched almonds to the smoothie base with a little extra water and top with a spoonful of natural low-fat yogurt, mixed with half a mashed banana or flavoured with a little finely chopped root ginger.

SERVES 1

110g/4oz/1 medium carrot, diced

1 dessert apple, cored but not peeled and diced

1 slice root ginger, quartered

Pinch ground cinnamon

125ml/4fl oz/½ cup water

1 tbsp cashew cream, see p33

For the topping

1 tbsp cashew cream, see p33

40g/1½oz/⅓ cup fruity cacao granola, see p30

1 medjool date, stoned (pitted) and sliced

Pinch ground cinnamon

½ small carrot, pared into thin ribbons with a vegetable peeler

Energy 328kcal/1380kJ; Protein 5.4g; Carbohydrate 57.2g, of which sugars 44g; Fat 10.1g, of which saturates 5.2g; Cholesterol 0mg; Calcium 78mg; Fibre 10.2g; Sodium 70mg.

POWER BALLS AND BARS

Snacks go super-healthy with these power-boosting bars and balls. Packed with wholegrains, nuts and seeds for sustained energy, plus added protein and fibre, they provide a healthy dose of vitamins and minerals. Choose from sweet potato brownie bars; cranberry, chia and apple muesli bars; blueberry and coconut wedges – or moreish fig and orange power balls and gingered apricot truffle balls.

Fig and orange power balls

MAKES 16

50g/2oz/⅓ cup unblanched almonds

½ tsp ground cinnamon

2 tsp hemp powder

2 tsp maca powder

1 tbsp ground flaxseeds

75g/3oz/½ cup mixed seeds, to include pumpkin, sunflower and sesame

100g/3¾oz/½ cup/or 5 dried figs

6 tbsp desiccated (dry unsweetened shredded) coconut

2 tbsp unsweetened hazelnut or cashew nut butter

Juice ½ medium orange

Little finely grated orange zest

We tend to forget about dried figs, choosing trendier medjool dates. Mixed with protein-boosting seeds these tasty snacks will boost flagging energy levels in a much healthier way than reaching for the biscuit tin.

1 Add the almonds to a food processor, screw on the lid and blitz until a coarse flour. Add the cinnamon, hemp and maca powder then the ground and whole seeds, figs and 4 tbsp of the coconut. Briefly blitz again until the seeds and figs are roughly chopped.

2 Add the nut butter and orange juice and blitz once more until the mixture begins to stick together.

3 Scoop heaped teaspoonfuls of the mixture on to a paper-lined baking sheet until you have 16 roughly shaped mounds. Roll the spoonfuls of mixture into balls in the palm of your hand then roll in 2 tbsp of coconut and the orange zest to coat. Pack into a plastic container, interleaving the layers with the paper, then seal and store in the refrigerator up to 3 days.

NUTRIENT NOTE Figs are full of natural sweetness and contain pectin, a form of soluble fibre which can help to reduce blood cholesterol levels and also insoluble fibre that aids digestion transit. Drying the figs concentrates the nutrients so making them a rich source of potassium with useful amounts of calcium, iron and magnesium. Seeds such as pumpkin, sunflower, sesame and hemp contain protein and are a good source of vitamins E and B as well as dietary fibre.

COOK'S TIP Maca powder is sometimes known as Peruvian ginseng and is regarded as an energy tonic in South America where it is also thought to help boost immunity and energy levels. It can be bought from health food stores, but simply leave it out if hard to find.

Per ball: Energy 7kcal/29kJ; Protein 0.15g; Carbohydrate 0.25g, of which sugars 0.23g; Fat 0.6g, of which saturates 0.2g; Cholesterol 0mg; Calcium 4mg; Fibre 0.2g; Sodium 0.5mg.

Flapjack cookies with ginger and turmeric

Made with reduced-fat and sugar, these gently spiced flapjacks are made with a small amount of soya margarine rather than butter, and maple syrup for natural sweetness, so are perfect for anyone following a vegan diet.

1 Preheat the oven to 180°C/350°F/Gas 4. Line two baking sheets with baking parchment.

2 Add the soya margarine, maple syrup and nut butter to a pan and heat gently, stirring until the margarine has melted.

3 Stir in the oats, quinoa flakes, spices and grated apple and mix well. Scoop out 16 heaped tablespoons on to the lined sheets. Flatten slightly with a fork then sprinkle with the sesame seeds.

4 Bake for 10–12 minutes until browned then leave to cool on the parchment. Transfer to a plastic container and store in the refrigerator up to 2 days.

NUTRIENT NOTE Turmeric is part of the same family as ginger and has long been used in Chinese medicine. It is a natural antiseptic and has anti-inflammatory properties that are thought to help with skin infections such as psoriasis, and also arthritis and possibly even Alzheimer's.

COOK'S TIP Some people following a gluten-free diet can tolerate oats, but always read the label as some processing plants also use wheat products so cross contamination may occur.

MAKES 16

75g/3oz/½ cup soya margarine

4 tbsp/¼ cup maple syrup

2 tbsp crunchy hazelnut or almond butter or unsweetened peanut butter

110g/4oz/1 cup jumbo rolled oats

40g/1½oz/¼ cup quinoa flakes

1½ tsp ground ginger

½ tsp turmeric

1 dessert apple, cored and coarsely grated, no need to peel

4 tsp sesame seeds

Per flapjack: Energy 6kcal/27kJ; Protein 0.1g; Carbohydrate 0.6g, of which sugars 0.2g; Fat 0.4g, of which saturates 0.1g; Cholesterol 0mg; Calcium 1.25mg; Fibre 0.06g; Sodium 2.3mg.

Chocolate popcorn bars

MAKES 10

1 tbsp olive oil

50g/2oz/¼ cup popping corn

110g/4oz/scant ½ cup
smooth unsweetened
peanut butter

3 tbsp coconut oil

100g/3¾oz dark chocolate
with 70% cocoa solids,
broken into pieces

2 tbsp maple syrup

For the topping
2 tbsp dried cranberries
2 tbsp dried goji berries
1 tbsp pumpkin seeds
1 tbsp sunflower seeds

Packed with concentrated energy these yummy all-American style popcorn treats are a twist on the usual cornflake or rice crispie refrigerator cakes.

1 Line a shallow 20cm/8in square cake tin or pan with a larger piece of baking parchment, snipping diagonally into the corners of the paper then pressing into the tin so that the base and sides are lined.

2 Heat the oil in a medium-sized pan, add the popping corn, cover with a lid and cook over a medium heat for 3–4 minutes, shaking the pan from time to time until all the corn has popped. Remove the lid and take the pan off the heat.

3 Add the peanut butter, coconut oil, chocolate and maple syrup to a second pan and heat gently, stirring from time to time until the chocolate has melted and the mixture is smooth and glossy. Take the pan off the heat then stir in the popped corn, discarding any kernels that haven't popped. Coat well in the chocolate then tip into the lined tin, roughly spread with the back of a spoon to level then sprinkle with the cranberries, goji berries and seeds.

4 Chill until set then lift the paper and popcorn mix out of the tin, peel away the paper and cut into 10 pieces. Wrap in paper and add to lunchboxes. Store in the refrigerator in a plastic container for up to 2 days.

NUTRIENT TIP Popcorn is a gluten-free wholegrain made up of three parts. The germ contains healthy oils, vitamin E, protein, some B vitamins and minerals. The bran contains most of the fibre, and the endosperm has starch, some protein and fibre. Homemade popped corn is healthy at just 32 calories per 1 cup of just-popped corn, it's what you add that can make it unhealthy so ditch the salt, butter and high sugary coatings.

COOK'S TIP The popcorn does soften the longer that you keep these bars for, so are best eaten on the day or next day of making.

Per bar: Energy 27kcal/90kJ; Protein 0.5g; Carbohydrate 1.7g, of which sugars 1.1g; Fat 1.6g, of which saturates 0.7g; Cholesterol 0.1mg; Calcium 1.4mg; Fibre 0.1g; Sodium 4mg.

Energy chocolate bark

SERVES 6

100g/3¾oz dark chocolate
with 70% cocoa solids,
broken into pieces

2 tsp maple syrup

1 tsp hulled hemp seeds

1 tbsp pumpkin seeds

1 tbsp sunflower seeds

25g/1oz/¼ cup mixed dried
fruit such as cranberries and
golden berries or goji berries

40g/1½oz/generous ¼ cup
mixed nuts to include
blanched almonds,
pecan and pistachio nuts,
roughly chopped

¼ tsp wheatgrass powder,
optional

There are some wild claims out there that dark chocolate can reduce blood pressure and stress, and even prevent cancer. While more research needs to be done to back up the claims, dark chocolate is an energy-dense food especially when mixed with healthy nuts, seeds and dried fruit. It is a good-mood food as it contains phenylethylamine, which is the same chemical that your brain creates when you feel as if you are falling in love.

NUTRIENT TIP Chocolate is high in calories so keep as an occasional treat rather than an everyday food in a healthy eating diet.

1 Melt the chocolate in a bowl set over a pan of gently simmering water then stir in the maple syrup. Spoon the chocolate on to a sheet of baking parchment set on a baking sheet and spread into a roughly shaped square about 20cm/8in with a palette knife.

2 Sprinkle the hemp, pumpkin and sunflower seeds over the chocolate then add the dried fruits and nuts and gently press into the chocolate with the back of a spoon. Sprinkle with the wheatgrass powder if using. Chill in the refrigerator for 30 minutes or longer if time, until set.

3 Lift the bark off the paper and break into shards. Store any leftovers wrapped in the baking parchment in a plastic box in the refrigerator up to 3 days.

Energy 30kcal/125kJ; Protein 0.5g; Carbohydrate 2.7g, of which sugars 2.4g; Fat 1.2g, of which saturates 0.7g; Cholesterol 0.16mg; Calcium 4mg; Fibre 0.3g; Sodium 0.8mg.

Gingered apricot truffle balls

MAKES 12

50g/2oz/⅓ cup mixed pumpkin and sunflower seeds

50g/2oz/ ½ cup jumbo rolled oats

100g/3¾oz/½ cup ready-to-eat dried apricots

2 tbsp dried goji berries

10g/¼oz root ginger, peeled and finely chopped

3 tbsp quinoa flakes

2 tbsp pressed cloudy apple juice

4 tsp hemp oil

4 tsp maple syrup

2 tsp raw cacao powder, for dusting

COOK'S TIP If you don't have any hemp oil then use olive oil or melt 4 tsp coconut oil and then stir into the mixture.

This healthier take on chocolate truffles is packed with slow-release carbs for sustained energy, and essential fatty acids and minerals.

1 Add the seeds and oats to a blender goblet or food processor and roughly chop. If using a blender, tip the mixture into a bowl then finely chop the apricots, goji berries and ginger and stir in with the quinoa flakes. Add the apple juice, oil and syrup and mix together with a spoon then your hands to make a coarse paste.

2 If using a food processor, add the apricots, goji berries and ginger to the chopped seeds and oats in the food processor and blitz until the apricots are chopped. Add the quinoa flakes, apple juice, oil and maple syrup and blitz again until the mixture binds together.

3 Divide the mixture into 12 even-sized mounds then roll in your hands to make small balls. Put the cacao powder on a sheet of baking parchment and roll the truffles in the cacao until lightly dusted. Store in a plastic container in the refrigerator up to 3 days.

Per ball: Energy 9.25kcal/27.5kJ; Protein 0.2g; Carbohydrate 0.97g, of which sugars 0.5g; Fat 0.3g, of which saturates 0.04g; Cholesterol 0mg; Calcium 1mg; Fibre 0.15g; Sodium 2mg.

Sweet potato brownie bars

Brownies are traditionally made with lots of melted butter and sugar – this healthier version is made with steamed sweet potato and mashed banana, with just a few tablespoons of maple syrup.

1 Preheat the oven to 180°C/350°F/Gas 4. Line a shallow 20cm/8in square cake tin or pan with a piece of baking parchment a little larger than the tin and snip diagonally into the corners of the paper then press into the tin so that the base and sides are lined.

2 Cook the sweet potato in the top of a steamer for 10–15 minutes or until just soft when pressed with a knife. Meanwhile add the dark chocolate, peanut butter, coconut oil and maple syrup to a small pan and heat gently, stirring until the chocolate has melted and the mixture is smooth. Take off the heat.

3 Transfer the sweet potato to a food processor, add the banana and blend until smooth. Add the vanilla and cinnamon then gradually mix in the eggs, one by one. Add the melted chocolate mixture and beat again until smooth. Mix the cocoa and baking powder together. Add to the food processor and blend again until smooth.

4 Spoon into the paper-lined tin. Sprinkle over three-quarters of the nuts and spread level then sprinkle with the rest of the nuts. Bake for 20–25 minutes until well risen and cracked around the edges with a slightly soft centre.

5 Put the tin on to a wire rack and sprinkle with a little extra diced chocolate, if using and leave to cool with the brownies still in the tin. Lift the paper and brownies out of the tin, peel off the paper and cut into 12 bars. Store any leftovers in a paper-lined plastic box in the refrigerator for up to 3 days.

MAKES 12

350g/12oz/or 2 small sweet potatoes, peeled and cut into chunks

50g/2oz dark chocolate with 70% cocoa solids, broken into pieces

3 tbsp smooth unsweetened peanut butter

3 tbsp coconut oil

3 tbsp maple syrup

150g/5oz banana, weighed in its skin, peeled and broken into pieces

1 tsp vanilla extract

½ tsp ground cinnamon

3 eggs

50g/2oz/½ cup unsweetened cocoa powder

1½ tsp baking powder

50g/2oz/scant ⅓ cup Brazil nuts, roughly chopped

25g/1oz dark chocolate, diced, to decorate, optional

Per bar: Energy 14kcal/59kJ; Protein 0.4g; Carbohydrate 1g, of which sugars 0.6g; Fat 1g, of which saturates 0.4g; Cholesterol 4.8mg; Calcium 3.25mg; Fibre 0.16g; Sodium 12mg.

Cranberry, chia and apple muesli bars

MAKES 12

250g/9oz or 2 small dessert apples, cored, no need to peel, and diced

2 tbsp water

2 tbsp coconut oil

150g/5oz/1½ cups muesli base, see p28

2 tsp chia seeds

2 tbsp dried cranberries

50g/2oz/scant ½ cup light muscovado (brown) sugar

1 egg, beaten

These tasty energy-packed low-fat muesli bars are sweetened with apples and just a little muscovado sugar, then mixed with the tiniest amount of coconut oil to keep them moist.

1 Preheat the oven to 180°C/350°F/Gas 4. Line a shallow 20cm/8in square cake tin or pan with a larger piece of baking parchment and snip diagonally into the corners of the paper then press down into the tin so that the base and sides are lined.

2 Add the apples, water and coconut oil to a medium pan, cover and simmer for about 5 minutes until the apples are soft. Mash the apples in the pan.

3 Stir the muesli, chia seeds and cranberries into the apple mixture then mix in the sugar and beaten egg. Tip into the lined tin and press into an even layer with the back of a spoon.

4 Bake for 30–35 minutes until golden brown. Mark into bars and leave to cool in the tin. When cold, lift the paper and muesli bars out of the tin, peel off the paper and cut into bars. Store in a plastic container in the refrigerator for up to 2 days.

NUTRIENT NOTE Tiny black chia seeds have grown hugely in popularity as they are rich in omega 3 fatty acids which is beneficial for brain function, lowering inflammation and for cardiovascular health. They are high in antioxidants and soluble fibre plus they contain calcium and some protein.

Per bar: Energy 12kcal/49kJ; Protein 0.3g; Carbohydrate 1.6g, of which sugars 0.9g; Fat 0.5g, of which saturates 0.2g; Cholesterol 1.9mg; Calcium 1.8mg; Fibre 0.2g; Sodium 2mg.

Blueberry and coconut wedges

These gluten-free wedges are made with just a hint of maple syrup and get their natural sweetness from the fresh fruity blueberries and banana. Often referred to as a superfood, blueberries are rich in antioxidants known as flavonoids which are thought to help protect the body from cancer, heart disease and premature ageing.

1 Preheat the oven to 180°C/350°F/Gas 4. Brush the inside of a 20cm/8in springform tin or pan with a little oil. Add the quinoa flakes, rice flour, cinnamon and baking powder to a large bowl then stir in the coconut and goji berries.

2 Mash the banana with a fork in a second bowl and beat in the eggs, vanilla and maple syrup. Melt the coconut oil in a pan until liquid then fork into the egg mix.

3 Pour the egg mix into the quinoa mix and stir together until well mixed. Add the blueberries and mix very briefly together then tip into the springform tin and gently press into an even layer.

4 Bake for 20–25 minutes until the top is golden brown. Take out of the oven, mark into 8 wedges and sprinkle with a little extra coconut, if liked. Leave to cool in the tin. Remove the wedges from the tin and enjoy while still slightly warm or cool completely and pack into a plastic box. Store in the refrigerator and eat within 2 days.

NUTRIENT NOTE Most of us are now familiar with wholegrain quinoa but it is also available in flaked form which can be made into porridge or can be added to cakes and bakes. Quinoa is one of the few vegetable sources that contains all 8 essential amino acids, making it a great protein booster for those cutting back on meat. It is also rich in fibre and minerals.

COOK'S TIP These wedges are made with gluten-free ingredients but always check the labels of different products before using.

MAKES 8

100g/3¾oz/generous 1 cup quinoa flakes

75g/3oz/½ cup brown rice flour

1 tsp ground cinnamon

1 tsp baking powder

25g/1oz/⅓ cup desiccated (dry unsweetened shredded) coconut, plus 2 tsp to decorate, if liked

2 tbsp dried goji berries

1 medium banana, about 200g/7oz unpeeled

2 eggs

1 tsp vanilla extract

4 tbsp maple syrup

50g/2oz/scant ⅓ cup coconut oil

110g/4oz/scant 1 cup blueberries

Per wedge: Energy 32kcal/107kJ; Protein 0.6g; Carbohydrate 3.9g, of which sugars 1.8g; Fat 1.03g, of which saturates 0.7g; Cholesterol 7.25mg; Calcium 3.5mg; Fibre 0.4g; Sodium 23mg.

Rocky-road almond energy balls

MAKES 24

75g/3oz/½ cup whole
unblanched almonds,
roughly chopped

50g/2oz/½ cup pecan nuts,
roughly chopped

150g/5oz/1 cup pitted dates

75g/3oz/generous ¼ cup
unsweetened smooth
peanut butter

3 tbsp maple syrup

110g/4oz/1 cup jumbo
rolled oats

1 tbsp sunflower seeds

2 tbsp pumpkin seeds

¼ tsp salt flakes

Packed with whole nuts, peanut butter, oats and maple syrup for concentrated energy, these have just a touch of salt to wake up the tastebuds. Add to small individual-sized plastic containers and keep in the refrigerator next to a healthy drink so that you add both to your sports bag or briefcase as you rush out the door.

1 Toast the almonds and pecan nuts in a dry frying pan for about 3 minutes, shaking the pan until lightly browned. Take off the heat and put to one side.

2 Add the dates to a food processor and blitz until finely chopped. Add the peanut butter and maple syrup and blitz again until a coarse paste. Add the oats and seeds and blitz together until only just mixed. Sprinkle in the warm nuts and stir together with a spoon.

3 Shape the mixture into 24 balls, put on to a baking sheet and sprinkle very lightly with a little salt. Cover with clear film or plastic wrap and chill in the refrigerator for at least 2 hours to firm up.

4 Pack the power balls into small plastic containers, seal and store in the refrigerator for up to 3 days.

NUTRIENT NOTE Nuts are a great source of protein, essential fatty acids plus useful amounts of B vitamins and minerals, but they are high in calories. Portion control is key, at 160–200 calories per 25g/1oz depending on type it is better to add nuts to a recipe rather than just graze on a bowl of nuts.

COOK'S TIP These balls are not for the kids in the family as the chunky nuts could be a potential choking risk and the added salt is definitely not recommended. To make child-friendly, double check that no-one has a peanut allergy, omit the salt, and finely chop the nuts and seeds when adding to the food processor.

Per ball: Energy 4kcal/18kJ; Protein 0.1g; Carbohydrate 0.4g, of which sugars 0.24g; Fat 0.25g, of which saturates 0.03g; Cholesterol 0mg; Calcium 0.75mg; Fibre 0.04g; Sodium 1.6mg.

Prune double deckers

Prunes have long been thought of as having a laxative effect, and if you are not a fan of high-bran cereals they make a much sweeter alternative. They are also rich in potassium which helps to maintain the fluid and electrolyte balance in cells and tissues and helps to regulate blood pressure.

1 Preheat the oven to 180°C/350°F/Gas 4. Line a shallow square 20cm/8in cake tin or pan with a larger piece of baking parchment, snip into the corners of the paper and press down to line the base and sides.

2 Add the prunes, water and vanilla to a food processor and blend until a coarse purée.

3 Melt the margarine in a medium pan then stir in the peanut butter and sugar. Mash the banana with a fork then add to the pan with the quinoa, oats and sunflower seeds. Stir the mixture together then spoon two-thirds into the prepared tin and spread into an even thickness.

4 Spoon the prune purée over the top and spread into an even layer then sprinkle with the remaining oat mixture and lightly press into the prunes. Bake for about 25 minutes until the top is golden brown.

5 Mark into 12 pieces then leave to cool in the tin. Remove from the tin, peel off the paper and pack into a plastic container. Eat within 2 days.

NUTRIENT NOTE Sunflower seeds are a useful source of vitamin E, B vitamins, and a range of minerals, protein and fibre. They are rich in energy-boosting 'good' unsaturated fats which does bump up the calorie count so eat little and often as part of a healthy diet.

MAKES 12

200g/7oz/1 cup ready-to-eat pitted prunes

6 tbsp water

1 tsp vanilla extract

100g/3¾oz/½ cup soya margarine

2 tbsp smooth unsweetened peanut butter or nut butter of choice

50g/2oz/⅓ cup light muscovado (brown) sugar

1 medium banana, about 200g/7oz unpeeled

100g/3¾oz/1 cup quinoa flakes

150g/5oz/1½ cups jumbo rolled oats

40g/1½oz/¼ cup sunflower seeds

Per bar: Energy 18kcal/74kJ; Protein 0.4g; Carbohydrate 25.3g, of which sugars 2.1g; Fat 0.9g, of which saturates 0.2g; Cholesterol 0mg; Calcium 1.8mg; Fibre 0.4g; Sodium 12mg.

Index